GOLF GIRL'S LITTLE TARTAN BOOK

Golf Girl's
LITTLE TARTAN BOOK

HOW TO BE TRUE TO
YOUR SEX AND GET THE MOST
FROM YOUR GAME

Patricia Hannigan

STEWART, TABORI & CHANG
NEW YORK

Published in 2010 by Stewart, Tabori & Chang
An imprint of ABRAMS

Library of Congress Cataloging-in-Publication Data:
Hannigan, Patricia.
  Golf girl's little tartan book : how to be true to your sex and get the
most from your game / Patricia Hannigan.
      p. cm.
  ISBN 978-1-58479-829-3
  1. Golf for women. I. Title.
  GV966.H36 2010
  796.352082--dc22

                        2009035982

Editor: Jennifer Levesque
Designer: Pamela Geismar
Production Manager: Tina Cameron

The text of this book was composed in Apricot, Avenir, and Century Light.

Printed and bound in China

10 9 8 7 6 5 4 3 2 1

Stewart, Tabori & Chang books are available at special discounts when
purchased in quantity for premiums and promotions as well as fundraising
or educational use. Special editions can also be created to specification.
For details, contact specialsales@abramsbooks.com or the address below.

THE ART OF BOOKS SINCE 1949
115 West 18th Street
New York, NY 10011
www.abramsbooks.com

Dedication

To my husband Nick, whose good-natured support for both my golf and this book has been unwavering and awesome.

CONTENTS

Introduction 9

The Mental Game:
Be Mistress of Your Emotions

Get Past Beginner 15

Let's All Be More Open-Minded 18

Work the Female Advantage 20

Revel in Those Red Tees 23

Be True to Your Style 26

Don't Keep Score 30

Don't Let the Purists Spoil Your Fun 33

Intuit Etiquette 36

Throw a Proper Tantrum 38

Learn to Laugh at Yourself 42

Embrace Distraction 44

The Physical Game:
Play Like a Girl

Carry a Big Stick—Just Hold Off Using It 49

Get Sticks for Chicks 53

Recognize that Nine is Fine 56

Play a Par-3 57

Get the Right Coach   60

Address the Ball with Your Derrière   65

Waggle Away   68

Love That Left Foot   70

Squeeze and Swing   73

Practice Like a Girl   76

Get Handicapped   80

Make Great Escapes   90

Play by the Rules (No Gimmes!)   93

Win by the Rules (No Cheating!)   99

The Social Game: Revel in Your Femininity

Sex It Up   103

Don't Act Your Age   106

Swing with Singles   110

Embrace Caddy Candy   114

Play with Your Man   117

Consider Club Membership   120

Play Nine, Then Dine   122

Indulge Your Fashion Fetish   124

Recover from Mortal Embarrassment   131

Epilogue

How I Shaved Five Strokes Off My Game   135

INTRODUCTION

Harvey Penick, whose *Little Red Book* is my golf bible, devoted his life to teaching others how to get the most from their game. A PGA Teacher of the Year, a World Golf Hall-of-Famer, and a coach to Ben Crenshaw, Mickey Wright, Kathy Whitworth, Betsy Rawls, Tom Kite, and Sandra Palmer, Mr. Penick was and still is revered for the simplicity of his wisdom—"Take dead aim" being a perfect example. He knew golf, he knew people, and he knew how to help people play better golf.

But one thing he didn't and couldn't know was what it's like to be a female trying to indulge her passion for golf.

Let's be honest. We women are confronted with a level of scrutiny men just don't have to deal with—and we get it from both men *and* women. It's not enough to play well. We often worry about how we look and what we wear, about how we behave and what we say. And no matter what we do to please our onlookers, to fit in at their clubs and competitions . . . we offend. Either we're too sexy in our appearance to be taken seriously as an athlete, or we're too athletic in our appearance to be admired as a female. Either we're way too aggressive in tournament play to be liked as women, or we're not aggressive enough to interest television audiences of mostly men. All sorts of stereotypes confront us out there on the fairways, seemingly contrived to send us packing. We can't drive far enough. We can't play fast enough. We'll never be *male* enough, we'd have to conclude, for men to cede any of their turf beyond one token week at St. Andrews R & A during the British Open.

Fact is, women can play golf just as well as men. Anyone remotely familiar with the etiquette and finesse integral to the game would have to conclude that it's rather perfectly suited to a feminine sensibility and skill set. But we girls are caught in the grip of a vicious swing, a *gotcha!* Catch-22. Observing how relatively few women are out there playing (one girl for every six guys), we feel self-conscious, intimidated, even unwelcome on the course; feeling unwelcome, we don't play, and *voilà!* Relatively few women are out there playing.

The problem, as I see it, is really one of female confidence. We women need to cultivate it for ourselves, which is why *Golf Girl's Little Tartan Book* hits the sweet spot. It isn't about golf so much as it's about playing golf on our own terms. We want to win at the mental, physical, and social game of golf *because of our sex*, not in spite of it. And we most certainly can, given our set of gender-specific traits.

I'll give you a perfect example. Not long ago, Scottish golf journalist John Huggan observed that in pitching, chipping, and putting, women should be every bit as good as men, but just aren't. For an explanation, Huggan sought out David Whelan, who's coached Paula Creamer, Rachel Hetherington, and other high-profile golf girls. Whelan pointed out that "far too much emphasis is put on hitting balls off the tee" by those coaching women, and "a lack of technique around the greens is the direct result." Whelan, who focuses his girls on the short game, is working to narrow what he perceives as "perhaps the biggest gender gap in golf."

Now why do so many coaches focus their female clients on driving? Because most every coach, being male, would naturally perceive hitting balls off the tee as the place for girls to start in order to overcome the handicap imposed by their less-powerful physiques. Men drive farther; women need to catch up to be competitors; ergo, women should work on their driving. But if I were to be coaching women, I'd focus on what we girls, with our precision and finesse, naturally excel at: The Short Game. I'd get girls just starting out to pitch and chip and putt until they could confidently compensate for whatever their driving might permanently lack. And that would show the men a thing or two. At some point we would probably have to insist that "the ladies' tee" be abolished, lest it give us girls too great a stroke advantage over the poor guys.

Coach Whelan went on to say that, from a coaching standpoint, women required more encouragement and individualized attention because they were inherently less confident than men. You might interpret his comments as sexist, but only if you thought that men's unreasonable and often unfounded confidence was a good thing. What's wrong with giving women the attention and encouragement they need, from a coaching standpoint, if they develop real confidence as a result? What's wrong with needing more nurturing, and more assurance? Like that's a *bad* thing?

And on the subject of confidence, let me say this. We like to look good, we girls. We know we're being watched; we know men can't help it. I'm not about to wear a bikini for my next foursome date, but you won't see me in boxy, baggy cuts or powdery pastels and prints, either. Because the styles, they are a-changing: Exciting colors, close-to-the-body cuts, and runway-inspired designs reflect the new thinking about girls in golf. Young pros like Natalie Gulbis, Paula Creamer, Cristi Kerr, and Michelle Wie now frequently take center stage at Fashion Week. Everybody, male and female, is beginning to "get it": We all play better, and we all sure have a lot more fun, if we girls get to indulge our yen for hot outfits and hip gear and stylish accessories. Golf is a social game, let's not forget—why wouldn't we bring to the party what every all-male party lacks?

And speaking of fashion, a word about that term "tartan." It's Scottish for what we call plaid, and it has long been associated with golf because the Highlanders who invented the game wore a lot of it. Fashion-wise, I'm very fond of tartan because its colors and patterns go way, way beyond the Burberry camel or navy-and-green Black Watch that usually come to mind. My new favorite skirt, for example, is a Pink Daiquiri blend in shades of Barbie fuchsia. But historically, tartan packs a lot of symbolic punch. Scottish clans wore tartans specific to their bloodlines, so that from a distance you could tell who was approaching by the pattern of his kilt or shoulder blanket. (My Irish ancestors, in fact, could be recognized a fairway away by their Hannigan plaid.) Scottish bloodlines, though, were matrilineal as well as patrilineal, meaning it was quite the honor, as a male, to wear your grandmother's family tartan. Clan chieftains, I've also learned, were as likely to be female as male. So while some people may perceive tartan as ancient and stodgy and male, it's really rather modern and fashionable and female.

Tartan symbolizes quite nicely, I think, what I'm aiming to do with this little book: Respect tradition but never be beholden to it. Tartan is sexy, golf is fun, and women belong in both! ☺

The Mental Game

BE MISTRESS OF YOUR EMOTIONS

GOLF IS A GAME OF SELF-CONTROL. No matter how good you get at the physical stuff—and there's lots to get good at—it's your "inner game" that ultimately matters the most: how centered you are, emotionally. (Watch Sergio Garcia bogey on the first hole of the playoff with Padraig Harrington during the 2007 Open . . . and then miss the final putt for birdie on the last hole.)

Which is why girls ultimately wield an advantage in golf over guys: We can hold it together better. We're not consumed from the get-go with illusions of our prowess. We're not laboring under ridiculous expectations. We can actually *enjoy* ourselves, no matter what our score. For us, golf is truly about the journey, not the destination.

Still, since we're so often playing the game with guys, it's easy to get infected by their competitive anxiety. Golf girls—especially those new to the game—tend to fret about course etiquette and club rules. They're prone to intimidation by men who play fast and loose and by women who won't let a ball go unmarked or a blade of grass get disturbed. They're not sure what to wear, where to tee off, or how to handle being teed off. In short, they're afraid of screwing up, and rather than risk embarrassment or discomfort, they'd just as soon quit.

This section addresses those fears with strategies to help you fend off anxiety, access inner calm, and tap into your innate female advantage.

GET PAST BEGINNER

*A*h, the beginning. In golf, as in love, beginnings are optimistic, and full of hope. They're unfettered by negative experiences or bad habits.

The thing is, though—with golf, anyway—the beginning is often too closely followed by the end. More often than in almost any other sport, those who pick up golf wind up dropping it. This premature ending thing is especially common when the beginning golfer is female.

Why is this? Well, there's the time element: eighteen holes ≥ four to five hours. We girls can do *that* math in our heads in a nanosecond, and here's what it adds up to: *I'm just too busy.* We are, after all, almost always busier than men. Their day is over the minute they're no longer being paid, whereas we're just starting in on the second shift. So a game that demands a four-hour chunk of leisure time is probably going to remain male-dominated.

And surely you've noticed: Golf culture is male dominated, in a big way. Go to any course and you'll see it. I'm talking about thirty-to-one ratios being totally average. Often it's more like fifty to one. We're just not used to that, even those of us who are bashing through glass ceilings every day. In real life we can't find such a wildly disproportionate ratio, even if we're trying hard to. (Some of us are really looking.) Still: Being the lone female among scores of men in the relaxed, familiar atmosphere of a lounge or club is one thing . . . and being the lone female in the competitive landscape of a golf course or even a driving range is quite another.

What's a golf girl to do?

First, don't waste precious time fretting about wasting other people's precious time out there on the course. Whomever you're playing with, they were all beginners once, too, and far from resenting you they'll be eager, as all addicts are, to get you hooked. Don't think that, just because you're a newbie and they're all good golfers that you're somehow a *burden* to them.

Most important, though, don't let self-consciousness cheat you of the chance to experience some moments of pure grace. I'll admit, the first time I went out, I was really worried about embarrassing myself, because the starting tee was right off of a crowded clubhouse deck. There were some foursomes of fearsomely macho men hanging around, and I could feel their eyes boring into me. However, I quickly realized that, despite my lack of skills (and I had absolutely none), golf is a game where you can *fake it 'til you make it*. When I'd hit a wormburner—one of many awful shots out there that first day— I'd just discreetly pick up my ball and move to where the foursome's best shot landed. Then I'd take my next shot from there. I didn't slow anyone down one bit. And amongst all the slicing drives and short putts, I managed to pull off some brilliant shots. I'd connect with the ball in such a way as to perceive just how incredibly good it would feel

Shank

This is a verb that describes what happens when you make contact with the ball (yay!) except not with the right spot on the club (boo!). Shanking the ball usually means you've hit it with the *hosel*, that slightly rounded joint where the clubface meets the shaft. The effect can be spectacular, with the ball spinning out to the extreme right or left at high speed. Not at all pretty. Golfers loathe this shot, especially those standing to the right or left of the shanker.

Wormburner

If you were a worm, you'd see why this shot might burn you: It's a shot that rips right above the grass or skids along the ground. Beginners are terribly prone to wormburners, as they have trouble getting their ball aloft. I hate this shot almost as much as the worms do.

to play well. Those moments of grace were what kept me playing, and got me past beginning, and inspired me to go out again and again . . . and again and again . . . despite the ever-present gallery of guys waiting to see "what that chick's gonna do."

Sure, you're going to make some really embarrassing shots. I still do. But here's what you'd see if you just lifted your head high: Golf is challenging and vexing enough to make a fool out of anybody, beginners and professionals alike. Just watch Phil Mickelson or Sergio Garcia in a major tournament and you'll see that your worst moment is by no means anything to be ashamed of (and you're not having it in front of millions of television viewers). Play for those few golden shots. Before you know it, those shots won't be so few. ☺

LET'S ALL BE MORE OPEN-MINDED

No Dogs or Women Allowed.

F or untold decades, this was the sign that hung outside the Royal and Ancient Golf Club house, the sport's most hallowed hall and home to its ruling body outside the U.S. The R & A, which presides over the six courses that comprise St. Andrews, is famously all-male, and has been for its entire 253-year history. But in 2007, for the first time ever, the Old Boys decided to let in the young professional women for the Women's British Open. More stunning yet, the Open was held on the Old Course, the most famous of St. Andrews' public layouts. And that awful sign came down.

Pretty remarkable, right? Even if it was for only a week in August, we girls got a room in *their* clubhouse. Everybody—competitors, caddies, and officials, both men and women (but still no dogs)—got to use the sacred male space during that golden tournament week.

We still have a long way to go, of course. It doesn't take long to bump up against that old "no dogs or women allowed" attitude, even if it isn't posted on a sign. Clubhouses may be "open," but just try calling up the to the pro shop to book a desirable tee time—you'll quickly find they're typically blocked out for the men. This works to intimidate us, which is why the male-female percentages in golf are still skewed wildly . . . which in turn perpetuates a self-fulfilling sort of segregation.

But when women infiltrate the Old Boys' clubs, even if only for a week, a subtle shift takes place in that male bedrock. We're inclusive by nature, we women: We don't want our "own" room, even if the men have theirs. We like mixed doubles and co-ed foursomes, and open-to-everyone nineteenth holes—and from what I've seen, so do men. When we leave the clubhouse, a certain social electricity leaves with us—and the men miss it.

I'm willing to bet that, as more fun, flirty, and fashionable women take to the fairways and greens, more men will be eager for us to inhabit the inner sanctum of their clubhouse, too. I see this as our mission, actually: not to break down the clubhouse doors, but to induce men to do it for us. I predict, in fact, that the notoriously exclusive Augusta National Golf Club will be inviting women to join its member rolls within five to ten years. Let's make it happen, girls: Take up golf and stick with it! ☺

WORK THE FEMALE ADVANTAGE

*A*s a rule, most women get pretty flustered when playing with men. We think—no, we *know*—they have the advantage, given how much farther they can drive. They're bigger and stronger than we'll ever be. They even putt better, due to the quality and quantity of instruction they receive at a formative age. So even before we get out there on the course with them, we're feeling inadequate, to the point of dreading the whole game.

But ladies: When it comes right down to it, we've got the *real* edge—because it's mental. In golf as in life, we can triumph over the taller, stronger gender by relying on the fact that men routinely overestimate themselves and underestimate us.

I actually came to understand "the female advantage" when I first started playing with men. Initially, I tried to avoid playing with anybody, venturing out in the chilly months of spring when the courses weren't crowded. But as soon as it warmed up, the men came out in droves, and before long I found myself shoehorned into a testosterone-fueled threesome, dreading my first tee shot. The guys, too, seemed less than enthusiastic to have me along. When I finally walked up to the tee, planted my feet, and drove my ball, the response from my new-found friends was a chorus of "Way to go!" and "*Nice* shot!" The thing is, it was a completely underwhelming drive. Straight and soaring, but most definitely way short. Meanwhile the boys lamented their own far more impressive efforts. This pattern continued throughout the round and by the time we sank our putts on the eighteenth green, I completely understood the female advantage.

What's frustrating, though, is how many women don't. Why do so many of us *give away our power?*

Ashley, a graphic designer I sometimes work with, is a good example. Out of the blue she called me up and *insisted* I meet her, *right now*, at the driving range. I didn't know her all that well, but since it was a good excuse to go out and hit golf balls, I headed right over. I found her in a bay at the far end of the building.

"Pat, you've got to help me," she pleaded, frantically sweeping at golf balls with her seven iron. Her shots were sputtering left and right along the ground, some hardly getting beyond the tee box. "I know you're into golf, and I need to be able to play well by next Thursday, I mean, *really* well, because I absolutely *need* this account."

Ashley, it turned out, was playing golf with the principals of a major ad agency that often awarded wonderfully lucrative projects to designers like herself. She had passed herself off as a very proficient golfer in order to be able to bond with the company honchos. "They're all men," she lamented, "and they're all really big golfers. Can you please help me get good?"

I could not fix her game in eight days, I confessed. But, I assured her, that didn't matter. "You have the female advantage," I said. And then, to prove it to her, I told her about Debbie Dahmer.

Debbie is a scratch golfer. She's won professional tournaments and made aces. She holds three course records in Southern California, probably because her amazingly long drives are matched

Scratch Golfer

A player whose handicap is zero, meaning, she plays to par. This is one very rare golfer. I happen to know exactly one: Year in and year out, hers is the name inscribed among the winners on the tournament plaque at Ridgewood Country Club.

only by her tremendous energy. And she happens to be tall, blonde, and curvaceous, which explains why, in 2004, Golf Channel's hit TV show *The Big Break* put the spotlight on her. She's used that attention to organize and host unique charity golf events all over the country.

At each of these events, Debbie sets up a "Beat the Pro" station. Golfers are invited to wager thirty dollars that they can beat the pro by hitting a better shot. If they do, they win a prize, plus "I beat the pro!" bragging rights. As Debbie wryly revealed, "When the pro they have to beat is a woman, most guys will underestimate what she can do and will jump at the chance to bet on their skill."

Needless to say, Debbie has raised a ton of money for charity this way.

"And that's the power of realizing men are their own worst enemies," I told Ashley. "You don't need to blow them away with your golf game, because even a mediocre shot is more than they expect from you. Not that you should ever play *down* to their expectations," I cautioned. "But by remembering they're focused on their own performance, not yours, you can play with confidence. And if you're confident, it doesn't matter how you play: the confidence is what they'll perceive and remember about you."

Ashley nodded. I think she may have even grasped it, because a couple of weeks later she sent me an email saying she'd gotten the account "thanks to 'the female advantage.'"

Don't underestimate it. You've got the edge; you've just got to use it. ☺

REVEL IN THOSE RED TEES

You're bound to hear it at some point: Women who hit from the ladies', or red, tees can't be viewed as legitimate competitors, because they have "an unfair advantage." My husband, for one, thinks it's outrageous that I get to hit off the forward tees and miss a couple of major hazards.

Don't believe it.

For starters, in case you haven't noticed, women are built differently from men. They tend to be smaller, slighter, and longer in the leg than the torso. Even the strongest female golfer—Anika Sorenstam immediately comes to mind—can't keep up, in terms of driving distance, with a guy like, say, Sergio Garcia. Red tees are simply an acknowledgment of this physical difference. They level the playing field.

Personally, I love the red tees. They give me confidence—something women and beginners can't get enough of. They've helped me avoid some terrible gullies, expansive water hazards, and deep roughs. Admittedly, avoiding some of the worst yardage on the course makes golf a completely different game . . . one I can really enjoy!

Still, I can understand how a lot of men, and even some women, get worked up about the red tees. I know a golfer who's a trader at Lehman (well, *was* a trader at Lehman) who insisted on playing off the white tees with the men. She just couldn't enjoy competing with them unless she, too, was shooting from the back of the box. Her score, naturally, wound up being somewhat higher. But before you feel sorry for her, consider this: She got a lot better at her game faster, because she got in a lot more practice. Every hole, she was forced to take an extra shot or two to make the green.

I've noticed, in fact, that amateur female golfers who play off the white tees are generally better than most amateur male players, for the very reason that they've gotten in way more practice. They've learned how to handle pesky ponds and hopeless bunkers, which a lot of recreational male golfers never take the time to master. White-tee women win at the club, if not on the pro circuit.

So now and then, in practice play, I'll hit from the white tees—to work in some extra shots, to work on my driving and fairway shots. But when the strokes count, I'm sticking to the red tees, because it makes me more valuable to the team. That's right: Men will invite me to join their threesome in tournament play for the very reason that I'm allowed to hit from the forward tees and miss some significant hazards. When we're playing Scramble, I'm a huge asset, because in this game, the longest shot from the tee-box acts as the new start point for the other three players to drop their balls and continue playing. With the red-tee advantage, I'm often the lead ball.

And guys—I know you have noticed this—*love* to win. As long as your red tee lets them take home that trophy, you'll not hear a word about the "unfair advantage" you have. Red tees *rock*! ☺

GOLF TERMS FOR WANNABES

chili dip to hit the ground behind the ball before striking the ball itself. Also known as a "fat shot," this is likeliest to occur when you're trying to chip—hence the association with chili dip.

dew sweeper a player in a pro tournament who, in the third or fourth round, gets assigned a very early tee time. Since early morning pairings on the weekend in a tour event consist of the players who've made the cut but are closest to the bottom of the field, "dew sweeper" is not a complimentary term.

air shot any attempt to strike the ball where the player fails to make contact, also commonly known as a whiff, or Big Whiff. It's counted as a stroke, unless you're playing with guys who can't bear to lose.

Kelly rule any rule a player attempts to impose during play that gives that player an advantage, or cancels out what otherwise would have been a disadvantage.

gimme a putt that all players agree should count automatically without being actually played (meaning, a putt so simple everyone can assume it wouldn't be missed). Gimmes are routine in casual circles, but are forbidden in stroke play.

BE TRUE TO YOUR STYLE

t a squelchy spring tournament in Montclair, New Jersey, I caught up with young LPGA star Morgan Pressel under an oversize golf umbrella. Play had been on-again/off-again due to the capricious weather, and Morgan, having only just finished a twice-delayed round, looked more like a soggy sailor than the preppy golf girl featured in Ralph Lauren ads.

"The weather was definitely a factor," she admitted when I asked about her several bogies (she had finished a dozen strokes back from the leader). "But you know what's the most distracting thing about playing in rain like this?" she added, sitting forward suddenly in her chair. "Having to *look* up to par, because neither the fans nor my sponsors want to see the golfer whose personal style they admire looking like a wet rag!"

Take my word for it: Even soaking wet, Morgan looked nothing like a wet rag with her sleek and preppy blonde pony tail tucked neatly into her hat. But her point really resonated: Women *are* watched in a way that men simply aren't. Knowing, at all times, that we're being judged on our appearance introduces a level of self-consciousness men simply don't have to contend with.

And you don't need legions of fans or sponsors to feel the pressure of being watched. Whether I'm playing a round with friends at the local muni or an important business tournament at an exclusive country club, I know my confidence can be compromised by something as simple as a raised eyebrow or frown from the low-handicap league matron who's focused on my hemline. If I step up to the first tee knowing there's a foursome of aspiring tigers waiting impatiently for their turn to bomb their drives, you bet I'm hoping my skort's not bunched in the back. Yes, that's what I'm thinking as I try like heck to remember, let alone concentrate on, my swing thoughts.

So what to do? Morgan has given this some thought. "Be true to your style, whatever it is," she advises, "and use it to create your own comfort zone. There's no set formula: It's what you feel good in. For some, that might be a short and close-to-the-body style, for others, it might be clothing that's athletic and less revealing. The important thing is that it's *yours*."

This advice brought to mind the time I played in a ladies' league with women who were uniformly better players than I was. I didn't particularly enjoy it, but not because they were more skilled: The issue was style—or their lack thereof. Their ensembles of oversize khakis and boxy white polos looked almost like a uniform, which may have been their intent. Each woman, too, accessorized with only a sensible white visor bearing the logo of a local bank. When I walked up in my comparatively diminutive pink-and-lime-green golf dress (with complementary bag and visor, of course), the reception was less than warm. "Aren't you colorful!" one gal blurted, rolling her eye for the benefit of the others. There were several sarcastic snickers directed at my lime-green golf bag, as well. I turned Lily-Pulitzer-pink. Yet, the interesting thing is, I played well. The uniformed ladies began to warm up to me.

The following week we gathered again to repeat our foursome. As a concession to them, I pulled on khaki capris and my roomiest polo. *And guess what?* I played terribly. I fit in, but I wasn't me—and *that* undermined my ability more than anything.

I told this story to Morgan and she laughed. "Whether it's a hundred-and-one degrees or cold, dank, and drizzly, as long as you're wearing what you feel good in, you're going to be less distracted."

I think James Enburn, a PGA Teacher of the Year who has worked with women golfers for over two decades, put it best when he said, "If a woman goes out there and tries to be someone she's not, she'll have a really hard time finding her own game." ☺

IN MY FANTASY FOURSOME:

Catherine Zeta-Jones

First, a leisurely round of eighteen holes on the sun-dappled fairways of the ultraprivate Bel-Air Country Club outside Los Angeles; then a late, relaxed lunch at the idyllic Top of the Tee grill. That's golf the way Catherine Zeta-Jones likes to play it when she's out with her girlfriends. The voluptuous, raven-haired actress is a big fan of the all-day golf date, which is one of the reasons I'd love to be one of her friends. But I think it's her solid appreciation for the statement a good golf accessory makes that's really endeared her to me. Catherine has been known to wear white cowboy hats and crystal-encrusted golf gloves while playing Bel-Air's infamously difficult par-70 course—my kinda golf girl. I can also relate perfectly to the dynamic she has with hubby Michael Douglas out there on the back nine: Like me she's inclined to give her man plenty of unsolicited advice, which, to his credit, he usually accepts. But like my husband, Michael has been known to tell her to shut up. That would explain those lovely golf accessories, no?

DON'T KEEP SCORE

on't even bring along a scorecard. Play the hole, win the hole. You'll have so much more fun, at least while your handicap is high.

The player who taught me the wisdom of this is Bonnie Banks. She joined Indian Hills Country Club in Marietta, Georgia, ten years ago in order to take up golf. She played alone at first, feeling slightly embarrassed at being an arch beginner, but the grounds keepers encouraged her and she pressed on. "I just fell in love with the beauty and the quiet of the course," she told me. "I loved the 'me time' those solitary rounds provided."

How's her handicap today, after joining a league and playing twice a week? "High, but holding steady," she laughs, tucking wisps of hair back under her visor. "I enjoy the challenge of self against par, but what I really love is the social aspect, the friendships I've made. And the exercise: Golf keeps me feeling energized and positive . . . and young!"

Which is no small thing, given that Bonnie is eighty-five years old.

In my experience, Bonnie is a terrific role model—not so much for taking up the sport at age seventy-five, but rather for sticking with it despite a lack of mastery. Many women seem to take up golf for a season, see little progress, and give up the game before ever even really getting started. They're like my blog readers, who often ask me online, "How can you enjoy something you're not good at?" They're so consumed with the struggle to lower their scores they miss out on the joy that Bonnie describes.

For women just starting out, the important thing is to remember that golf is a *game*, not a test. Men tend to view it as a test, but that doesn't mean you have to suffer alongside them. (Or cheat, which is what they do when, after insisting on keeping score, they find they're just not playing well.) In fact, see if you can find other women to play a golf game with you—Splashies, Snakes, and Shoot-Out, to name a few—as opposed to a game of golf. Lots of lady golfers in my circle confess they're playing golf games as often as they were playing rule-book golf, and really enjoying it. In my book, you're only playing a great game if you *keep* playing it . . . well into your eighties. Bonnie, you *go*, girl! ☺

REASONS TO LOVE GOLF
EVEN IF YOU'RE TERRIBLE

Shots that defy the laws of physics

Fresh air and the Great Outdoors

Meeting new people

Hanging with old friends

Swearwords you've never heard before

Conversations about balls, shafts, and strokes

Rare wildlife sightings

Guy candy

Ian Poulter

Flippy pleated skirts

Spouting whales on captains of industry

Winning bets with a 42 handicap

Other people's sheer athleticism

Riding around in a cart

Nineteenth (drinking) hole

DON'T LET THE PURISTS SPOIL YOUR FUN

Have you met Little Miss Marker? The Divot Diva? Or any of the Play-Through Boys?

If you haven't yet, trust me—you will. Rules characterize every sport, but in golf, according to a certain group of individuals who feel morally obliged to enforce them, even during recreational rounds.

Don't get me wrong: I like that golf has its own etiquette, because a lot of players out there could use better manners, both on and off the course. But this group of sticklers—the Purists, I call them—has another agenda in mind. Male or female, young or old, the consistent characteristic of all self-described Purists is their need to make sure that golf *not be perceived as fun*, because if you're having fun, you're just not taking the game seriously enough.

The best way to keep these people from being a royal pain in the golf pants is to see them coming so you can anticipate their neurosis. Here are the ones to watch for:

Little Miss Marker—For some reason, this Purist is frequently female (though I've met a number of Little Misters as well). She's fine on the fairways; it's on the putting green you had better mark your ball, or woe betide you. Even if your ball is yards away from any trajectory her ball could conceivably take, mark it or risk a blistering comment. I've got a couple of crystal-studded markers I bring out on just this sort of occasion. Little Miss Marker frowns on flashy ball markers as being altogether too frivolous; she generally uses a tarnished brown penny. But hey—it's because of her that you need a marker in the first place.

Divot Diva/Divot Don—A close relative of Little Miss Marker, DD scours every green for the slightest dimple of a divot and then, with a grimace and scowl, whips out a special repair tool and ostentatiously repairs the offending bit of turf. God forbid you disturb three blades of grass on the green, or DD will fix you with a stare that will have you dropping to your knees with your own tool. I have a couple of divot fixers that match my ball markers, so I'm ready to show just how responsible I am.

Divot

- the patch of turf your iron scrapes up when you swing at a ball on the fairway
- the rut in the fairway created by your scraping iron
- the dimple in the green where your ball landed

Divots can actually tell you something about your swing, too. If you scrape up turf just in front of where the ball was at rest, that means your club struck the ball first, then the ground—a "good divot." If, on the other hand, you dig up turf behind the ball, that means you hit the grass first—a "fat shot." Either way, you owe it to the course and other golfers to repair your handiwork, usually by retrieving the bit of turf and tamping it back in place. If you can't replace the sod, then repair the bare spot with a sprinkle of the grass seed mix provided at every hole. To repair the indentation your ball made when it landed on the green, use a divot tool to lever up the depression until the grass is perfectly level again.

Playing Through

As a beginner you will quickly become familiar with this term, as the golfers behind you will ask if they may "play through." This simply means suspending your play so that they may go ahead of you, since they're playing faster. The optimal time to yield to their request is on the tee, before you set up your drive. Otherwise, it's annoying for them and hugely distracting for you to have them hanging about impatiently while you attempt to concentrate on your swing thoughts. Feel free to invite pesky foursomes to play through if they don't suggest it first.

The Cart Micro-Manager—I know such a Purist personally. She actually took a *full-day class* in Cart Management. I had no idea carts needed managing, let alone by someone with a Masters in the subject. But it turns out they do, especially when you go to park them. Count on the cart manager to tell you why, exactly, your cart is in violation of course rules, being parked two feet beyond the line or with its wheels turned four degrees past optimum. Better to just let her drive.

The Play-Through Boys—The play-through gene is distinctly male. It manifests itself on the first tee, usually with imploring eye contact. With every hole that you advance, the look these boys give you gets more menacing—even if they're struggling to keep up. That's what's so weird about these Purists: They don't know what kind of player you are but they always imagine they're way better. I say, let them play through whenever you can, even if—*especially* if—there's a slow foursome right ahead of you. You don't want to keep looking up to see their open disdain. ☺

INTUIT ETIQUETTE

"*I*t's all this business about *the rules* that gets me uptight," my friend Amanda insists. "I feel like everyone else grew up knowing exactly where to be on the tee and who hits next on the fairway and how to handle the flag for a member of your foursome and all that etiquette stuff. Everyone but *me*."

To my way of thinking, golf etiquette is pretty intuitive. As long as you're sensitive to others' needs—and that's our defining trait as women, right?—you'll know how to behave out there on the course, or at least, you'll know how not to offend.

It seems pretty obvious, for instance, that when someone's about to drive off the tee, you should be well out of her space. Likewise, most women I know instinctively go quiet when someone on the green is trying to concentrate on her putt. A lot of golf is just the golden rule spelled out: Do unto others as you would like them to do unto you.

But inevitably, we will meet up with an Etiquette Dominatrix, who gets all bent out of shape when you don't intuit where to leave the cart or how to prop your bag. Not only does this kind of golf partner get us uptight, she also ruins our good time—perhaps even to the point where we just don't want to venture out there again, for fear of offending. We women are sometimes *too* sensitive to others' needs.

The best defense against this sort of pressure, I've found, is to mount a good offense: Present yourself as a bit of an etiquette cynic from the start. If you're playing with finicky friends, reinforce the idea of a relaxed game each time you head out. If you're playing with a new group, introduce yourself and add something like, "You know, I'm a beginner, but I'm really passionate about this game. I just love to have fun with it, so I'm not a stickler for some of the more mundane rules *[smile, eye roll]*. But if there's anything on the course that drives you crazy, please let me know. I'll do the same. Otherwise, let's just enjoy it."

That way you've turned it around to make the Stickler feel that you're the one who's accommodating her (or him), not vice versa.

Now, if you're playing St. Andrews or you're a guest at Augusta National, you're entitled to feel intimidated by club and course rules: Everything about these holy shrines and inner sanctums is meant to intimidate you. But I'm guessing that if you're a beginner, you're not yet getting those invitations. So take it easy. A relaxed attitude, you'll find, is contagious. ☺

THROW A PROPER TANTRUM

*L*orena Ochoa will slap her right thigh. Paula Creamer sometimes spanks her putter. Morgan Pressel has been known to pout and cry.

You'll see it, sooner or later, even among the pros on the LPGA: a tantrum. A bit of bad behavior. Some acting out.

However, you'll notice that the women are admirably controlled, compared to the men. World Hall of Fame golfer Tommy Bolt's meltdowns were so memorable he became known as Thunder Bolt. He threw his clubs. He took revenge on putters by tying them to the back of his car and driving home. Once, narrowly missing the hole multiple times in a row, Bolt gestured wildly at the sky and demanded, "Why don't you come down here and fight like a man?"

The question isn't whether or not to throw a tantrum—it's *how.* Bolt, for instance, admitted that at first he threw clubs because he was angry, but ultimately made it part of his show. "I learned that if you helicopter those dudes by throwing them sideways instead of overhand, the shaft wouldn't break as easy," he observed. "It's an art, it really is."

And that's what makes a *proper* tantrum: Ultimately, you're in control. You vent just enough energy and emotion to clear your head, not lose your top.

I remember my first tantrum. I'd gotten through my whole first season without incident; after all, I was a beginner, and this was a new adventure. Frankly I expected to excel at golf, having excelled at both field hockey and gymnastics in high school. I spent the winter months, following that first season, hitting endless golf balls indoors at a heated range and working each week with a private coach. In the evenings I would practice putting on my Persian carpets for hours. When the spring came round I had improved substantially; I felt pretty smug. Even my highly critical husband, who's well known for his backhanded compliments, declared, "I'm impressed, this year I'll actually be able to enjoy playing with you."

But golf has a way of punishing smugness. Three rounds into the season, I had a bad day. For some reason, I could no longer accept the whiffs and worm burners. Each one angered me more, until, by the time we reached the turn, I was seething. We took a quick break in the clubhouse and, while waiting to grab a couple of Coronas, I did what women are socialized to do: I took a deep breath and began reciting positive statements to replace my negative self talk. By the time we were ready to tee off on the back nine, I felt substantially more relaxed. But then came my terrible tee shot, followed by a couple of fairway flubs and a chip right into the rough. The whole effort culminated in a frightful four-putt. And you know what I did? I took a page from Paula's book and spanked my putter. Spanked it really hard and scolded it. That was my meltdown. I felt better immediately and played better for the rest of the round.

My theory is, women actually benefit from some of the very elements in our upbringing that can seem so detrimental in the boardroom or in other competitive sports. We feel anger, sure. But we can master it—a vital skill in golf, probably the most vital in terms of the mental game. It's our ace in the hole, really, because golf pushes *all* the buttons. And men—just watch Sergio Garcia, or Colin Montgomerie or even, at times, Tiger Woods—let their anger get the better of them. They seem to think it will help. In a recent study conducted at Southwest Minnesota State University, researchers found that men felt less effective and less instrumental when forced to hold their

Foozle

I love this made-up word, not because I made it up but because I get to use it so often. A foozle is simply a bungled shot. I find it especially descriptive for those shots that no one can explain, the ones that go backward or straight up in the air or zing off into the parking lot. Foozle just *sounds* like an ugly shot, don't you think?

anger in, whereas women didn't feel nearly as constricted when they didn't express their anger directly. *Golf Digest* distills the data further, reporting that men are eighteen times more likely than women to break a golf club in anger on the course, whereas women are nineteen times more likely to cry. Both sexes swear in almost equal amounts— listen to Cristina Kim sometime—but men tend to drink and gamble more during a round. Almost half of the men (forty-seven percent) admitted to getting into a "verbal confrontation" with other golfers on the course versus twenty-seven percent of women.

So ladies, when you're having one of those rounds where the tee shots are shanking and the four-putts are rolling and every fairway shot is a foozle . . . when you feel like you want to throw clubs, punch your playing partner, or tear up the entire golf course, here's my advice: Act like a lady. Reap the reward of all that conditioning you probably received as a little girl. Spank that putter, use a spicy expletive or two, but *control your anger.* Despite what you've heard from your therapist or Dr. Phil about expressing your rage, the ensuing adrenaline surge will almost always do you in on the golf course.☺

GOLF GIRLS I ADMIRE:

Jeanne Carmen

She was an American original. Born at the dawn of the Great Depression, Jeanne ran away from small-town Arkansas at the age of thirteen for a glittery life on the road—a road that took her to Broadway and Vegas, Hollywood and Scottsdale. A model, a pin-up girl, and a B-movie star, she was also the first female trick-shot golfer and golf hustler, a "natural" who shot 80, playing barefoot, in her very first round (with singer Perry Como!). She gave lessons to Marilyn Monroe and Jayne Mansfield; she dated Clark Gable and Elvis Presley. Many who saw her tried to convince her to go pro. Lana Turner and her husband even financed Jeanne's membership at the famous Riviera Country Club. But Jeanne was a free spirit who had no taste for the discipline and dedication professional golf required. She loved doing her trick-shot act but she hated playing on course.

Jeanne managed to make a pretty good living in Hollywood as the platinum-blond "Queen of the B-Movies," but wound up living a quiet life in Arizona as a brunette with a husband and three children. In her last interviews, Jeanne always said that it was golf that gave her the most joy in her life.

LEARN TO LAUGH AT YOURSELF

ou swing big . . . and fail to make contact. You go to chip, and somehow the ball winds up going . . . backward. You try to sink a putt . . . and shoot your ball right off the green.

It's going to happen. And even if you want to flee into the woods or hop in the cart and make a speedy exit, don't. Laugh loud, and laugh first. You'll be amazed what a tension reliever this is, and not just for you.

Keri Murphy knows all too well the wisdom of this strategy. A former model, two-time Miss Oregon contestant, and Miss America coach, the Portland resident is president and owner of Wilhelmina MTG, a model and talent agency. You can catch her girl-next-door good looks on cable TV, too, most recently as host of *Highway 18*, a golf reality show on the Golf Channel. And you can see her every day online at GolfNow TV, where she hosts a daily golf trivia show. But for all these accomplishments, Keri is best known by her fans for . . . messing up.

First, there's the GolfNow TV Keri Blooper Reel of the Month, or even, the Best of Keri '08. The site's three-minute clips feature Keri flubbing her lines, mispronouncing a famous golfer's name, making weird noises, or just drawing a blank. Most of the comments posted on the site don't even talk about the trivia answer or the prize: they instead rave about how engaging Keri is when she blows it.

Then there's her golf game. Keri is far from a scratch golfer. Very, very far, in fact. No one knew this until, as host of *Highway 18*, she found herself as the celebrity guest golfer in a charity tournament with three businessmen, all expert golfers. "I realized that because I was hosting a Golf Channel show, and representing a golf-club line, everyone just assumed I was quite good," Keri explains. "Well, I had only played a couple of times in my life at that point. I missed shot after shot. The few I did hit didn't go far, or straight." Keri rolls her eyes at the memory. "The guys couldn't hide their surprise at my limited skills, but at least they were nice about it. I was mortified."

Since then, Keri has made progress. She's taken lessons, put in hours at the range, and persevered even when she felt like quitting—"which I would have done, except I didn't have the option: Golf outings and events were *so* part of my job." Still, what's made the biggest difference in her game, she says, is her ability to laugh at herself. "I finally accepted two things," she says. "First, golf is just not a sport I'm going to learn quickly. And second, the more fun I *seemed* to be having, the more fun I actually had out there."

So if Keri can whiff big in front of national TV cameras and enjoy Blooper fame all over the worldwide net, you can surely learn to whoop with amusement the next time you foozle in front of a few of your friends. ☺

Chip

A chip, or chip shot, is one you make with a "lofted" club, generally a 9-iron or pitching wedge. The loft, or extremely flat angle, of the club head sends the ball more up than out, making it the shot to use when you're trying to close a short gap between the rough and the green. The idea is to swing and strike with your weight on your back foot, so that the ball pops up and plops down on the green close to the hole. The greater the loft, the more plop, and the less roll, you can expect. The pros make this shot look easy, but in truth it takes a *lot* of practice to perfect.

EMBRACE DISTRACTION

Scottish golfer Colin Montgomerie is famous for two things: He's never won a major championship, finishing second on five occasions; and he cannot tolerate distraction, which may explain why he is golf's most famous runner-up. For this guy, a babbling two-year-old, a camera lens stationed in the wrong spot, or the looming presence of a television anchor has been enough to put him off his game—quite literally. Years ago in New York he refused to hit his ball until the crowd went dead silent, implying it was *their fault* he wasn't playing up to par.

Most veteran players, amateur as well as professional, accept distractions on a golf course as part of the game. They've learned how to tune them out, and they've got plenty of suggestions on how you can, too. But I have a rather different, rather *female* bit of advice for you: Don't focus past distraction. *Embrace it.*

Last summer on a road trip across New England I had the opportunity to play at Prouts Neck Country Club, an awesome links course in Scarborough, Maine. The day was crystal clear, but the winds were whipping and, to make matters worse, I had agreed to play with some experienced (i.e., impatient) links players, three men I hardly knew.

The round began inauspiciously. I foozled my first tee shot, really quite badly. The most curmudgeonly of the group muttered something under his breath. Tension rose as my successive shots showed no sign of improvement. I felt myself beginning to assume the dreaded role of golf victim, obsessed with my sloppy shots and compelled to

Links

Here in the U.S. we refer to almost any course that's relatively treeless as "a links course." Marketers have compounded this inaccuracy by using *links* as an upscale substitution for *golf course*, as though playing golf is infinitely superior or somehow more authentic when it's played on links.

In fact, the term refers quite specifically to land that links coast and farmland—the land that, back in the United Kingdom, golfers quickly appropriated for their game. The Scots, who are credited with inventing the sport of golf, must have figured that the links weren't much good for agriculture, being rather sandy and windswept. Because of this longstanding association between golf, sand, and water, American golf courses made a point of incorporating water hazards and sand traps, to replicate the challenges, if not the scenery and salt spray, of those original links courses.

make more of them. Nine holes in, I actually contemplated quitting.

But then I caught sight of a lone red-throated loon, a spectacularly large and rare species of water fowl known for its hair-raising call. Against the cobalt blue sky, its thin bill tilted slightly upward as it rode low over the coastal waterway, it was an enchanting sight that filled me with a kind of giddy delight. The overambitious tee shot I had just hit, which the winds had carried directly into the salt marshes, fell from my mind as I watched this magnificent bird glide across past juniper, holly bushes, and jagged gray rocks.

Did I lose my focus? You bet. I dropped all thought of golf, or at least, all memory of my bad shots and my growing angst. But even the guys, with the exception of the curmudgeon, took notice. "Looks like a Winslow Homer painting," one of the guys said, gesturing toward the horizon. "This is why we play golf," the second responded, smiling at me. The curmudgeon just kept on muttering (some golfers can't let go, no matter what), but it no longer mattered. My mood had been lifted by this unexpected encounter. I began to feel much more in sync with myself; on the back nine I even found ways to use the unique coastal landscape to my advantage.

The point is, what some might call distraction—a blustery wind, sun glinting off water, the cry of a loon—is what we girls might consider to be the whole reason for playing. The natural beauty I encounter on a golf course is enough to take my thoughts off my game and *give me a whole new perspective* on it. Just the other day, in fact, seizing a late-afternoon opportunity to play nine holes on my bedraggled little municipal course down the street, I looked up from retrieving my ball and there was a perfect red fox, standing frozen at the edge of the course. There was no dramatic seascape to be seen, no breathtaking vista of perfectly manicured greens; just a strange spectator poised on an expanse of scraggly grass. But I was enchanted, all the same—my number-one reason for taking up the sport and sticking with it. ☺

The Physical Game

PLAY LIKE A GIRL

GRACE PARK. PAULA CREAMER. Anna Rawson. Carin Koch. Natalie Gulbis.

If playing like these women is playing "like a girl," then I daresay a lot of men wish they could. Fact is, we're good at this game *because* we're female. Our slighter builds, our bumps and curves, our tendency to favor precision over power, and our ability to listen and learn—everything, in short, that makes us distinctly feminine makes us singularly formidable out there on the golf course.

Which is why what works for men isn't necessarily what works for us. We benefit from a 7-iron more than a driver, a par-3 course rather than a driving range, and a fun golf game over a highly competitive round. In addition, what men think we should do to improve our game isn't always in our best interests. We're going to play nine holes, not eighteen; we're going to wiggle as well as waggle; and when we address the ball, we're going to stick out our derrière, not obsess about target lines. We practice differently, swing differently, and, as it turns out, score ourselves differently (as in, we don't cheat). On an intuitive level, Golf Girls know what works for them. This section's about putting all of that intuition into actual play.

CARRY A BIG STICK—
JUST HOLD OFF USING IT

When I arrived at my first golf lesson a couple of years ago, with fourteen clubs in my bag, I was told to grab my 7-iron. "You won't be needing the others for a while," my instructor added.

I had no problem with this approach. With my trusty 7, I began consistently hitting straight shots of about seventy-five yards. Then one day out on the range, I couldn't help but notice that the young men on either side of me were *thwakking* balls well past the 200-yard marker. My scrawny 7-iron was no match for their oversize drivers.

Had I been ill-advised by my otherwise excellent instructor? Did he think women weren't capable of handling a club that wielded so much power?

Before my next lesson I was determined to find out. Picking up my long-neglected driver, I took a couple of practice swings. The length! The heft! I felt instantly empowered. I stepped up to the rubber tee, fully expecting I'd be meeting that ball with a 7-iron swing *on steroids*.

Plink. The ball scraped along the ground and came to rest about forty-five yards out—a classic worm-burner. Repeated attempts produced nothing better. Worse, when I finally gave up, exasperated, and went back to my 7-iron, *it* no longer worked for me, either—as though it resented my infidelity, and was taking its revenge.

At my next lesson, my instructor immediately knew about my dalliance. "I told you NOT to use your driver for a reason," he admonished. "Now you'll need to build your confidence back up."

Since then, of course, I've learned to use my driver almost as well as my 7-iron. I can drive the ball maybe 150 yards fairly consistently. But like most women, I have sort of a love/hate relationship with my Big Stick, and I wonder: Was this just sexist conditioning? Or was my coach correct in steering me away from it as a beginner?

At age four, Michelle Wie was consistently driving a golf ball 100 yards. She'd only just started playing, too, with a set of junior clubs her parents had given her. The set consisted of a driver, a 5-iron, a 7-iron, and a putter. According to her dad, the first club she hit with was the driver. "I mean, from the *beginning* she chose the driver," B.J. Wie says of his daughter. "And she tried to hit the ball really hard."

B. J., who is frequently maligned for pushing his daughter too hard, would surely not have been criticized for his approach had Michelle been a Michael. Boys, after all, are continually encouraged to "bomb it" with the driver, no matter what their stroke or swing is like. One sees ample evidence of this on any golf course, as young men prowl the woods in search of their errant balls. And given how Michelle turned out, it appears B. J. was right: Give a girl a driver from the get-go and she'll become, like most men, a power hitter.

But then there's Liz, the wife of my family physician and a champion player at our club. She started playing three years ago, at the age of forty-eight, with a beginner set of clubs her husband, a scratch golfer and four-year club champion, had given her—after he'd removed the driver. "I wanted to make sure she learned how to control her swing," he explained, "before she grabbed that big club and started doing things that could shatter her confidence."

As patronizing as that sounds, I've come to perceive that he wasn't being sexist, any more than my instructor was. And here's why: the driver has the least amount of loft. To get the ball lifted into the air, you've got to give it a certain amount of head speed—not an easy thing to do with your longest club. Anything less than a powerful swing and your ball is likely to stay low. Also, any crazy curvy thing your club does to the ball is magnified when you do it with your driver.

So Michelle notwithstanding, most instructors agree: The best approach to take with girls and boys—or forty-eight-year-olds of either sex—is to hold back on the driver. The vast majority of beginners benefit from the confidence and consistency that's built with a good command of irons.

And my club of choice? Now that I've been playing for three years, I've come to see the importance of having a close, intimate relationship with that least sexy, least powerful, but ever faithful little wand: my putter. Like most long-term affairs, there's not much to say about it. As with a spouse, the more time you spend with it, the more you come to appreciate its virtues. Sure, driving can be fun. But like a lot of male fetishes, it's frankly . . . overrated.

So carry a big stick, but hold off using it until you can be sure all that power will take you where you want to go. Good advice for golfers *and* politicians, I think. ☺

GOLF TERMS FOR WINNERS

birdie finishing a hole in one stroke under par. Apparently a couple of guys playing the Atlantic City Country Club in 1899 coined the term after one of their party hit a bird on his first shot and then dropped his second shot inches from the hole. Since he wrapped up the par-4 hole in three shots, his buddies dubbed this miracle "a birdie," and since many tourists played that country club, word got out.

eagle finishing a hole two under par. An eagle is a "big birdie," after all.

albatross finishing a hole in three under par. Like the legendary big white seabird, this is quite a rarity.

GET STICKS FOR CHICKS

When I took up golf, pretty much on a whim, the first thing I did was run over to our discount department store and buy myself a ready-made set of ladies' clubs. The set included everything I could possibly need to get started—woods, irons, putters, hybrids—along with a really cute bag. (Never underestimate the importance of a really cute bag to your confidence and, therefore, competence.) I improved my game with these clubs, even though a close friend of mine insisted that this wasn't possible. "You want to buy the very best gear you can afford," she clucked.

I didn't see it that way, and I still don't. Confidence, I would argue, is what makes the biggest difference in a girl's game—not high-end gear.

But about a year into playing, I found myself shelling out the big bucks for—you guessed it—a driver. I had seen first-hand the difference a good driver could make. I could even hear the difference, on impact—that toneful *thlock* of the ball hitting the head on its sweetest, hottest spot. My friends let me try theirs a few times during their rounds, and I could soon feel the magic of their wands. I wound up getting a Cleveland HiBore, and I have not regretted the investment. I won't pretend to know the relevance of its MOI (Moment of Inertia), CGP (Center of Gravity Projection), or OLC (Optimum Launch Conditions); what I do know is that it makes a really satisfying sound when it meets the ball dead on, and I'm getting more distance and greater precision than I thought myself capable of. It's got a great cover, too.

The next thing I upgraded was my sand wedge. I had to: I lost the one that came with my beginner set. Since Cleveland had been so good to me I decided to get the CG 11—the 56-degree, standard bounce model in pink. It's renowned for its stability and "extra forgiveness," and who can't benefit from that? I just know it will be my scoring club . . . when I learn how to use it.

Lastly, I caved to peer pressure and bought myself a really decent putter. There are many; the one I chose is the GEL Sapphire, partly because of its swanky color scheme (it's black with pink accents). I'm particularly fond of its oversize mallet and its pink alignment guides, because I can really see when I've got the ball headed in the right direction. I love the way it's weighted, too. And the Winn grip happens to match my favorite golf shirt.

And that's it, investment-wise. You can spend tons of money on all your clubs, but remember that 75 percent of your game will depend on just three: driver, wedge, and putter. Spend what you need to feel confident with these essentials, and you'll have everything you need to succeed on the course—and plenty of budget left over to invest in matching outfits. ☺

GOLF GIRLS I ADMIRE:

Ivanka Trump

*L*ike father, like daughter. A *summa cum laude* graduate of the University of Pennsylvania Wharton School of Finance and vice president of real estate development and acquisitions for the Trump Organization, Ivanka Trump is no slouch in the business world. Not everyone knows, however, that she's just as hard-working in golf circles. Maybe it's Dad's Scottish heritage; maybe it's because she is managing development of a golf course in Aberdeen, Scotland, among other Trump projects. But it's by no means all business. "I love being with a bunch of friends, playing a game that's competitive but that encourages you to be a better person," she confided in a recent interview. Certainly she looks good out there on the links: At five-foot-eleven, she's statuesque, to put it mildly. Calloway must have thought so, too, since they made her a spokesperson. (That's got to be a good alliance for any golf girl, but especially one who needs extra-long clubs.) The combination of brains and beauty must be rather intimidating to anybody hoping to close a billion-dollar deal out there on the fairway. Could it be that Ivanka is the secret to her father's success?

RECOGNIZE THAT NINE IS FINE

Time, as I've mentioned, is not what we girls have a lot of. But you don't need to find yourself a four-hour window to sneak off with your bag and cleats. Because you don't need to play eighteen holes.

Nine is fine. The purists will disagree, but they always do. Think about it: You can party hard Saturday night and sleep in Sunday morning. You can take advantage of those last daylight hours on a weekday evening. You can even justify it as a working lunch, depending on whom you take along and what you talk about. Guys do business on the back of the tee all the time. We can, too—and still have the whole afternoon to get everything else done back at the office.

Fact is, when I've got a lot on my desk, I just can't enjoy four or five hours on the course. I'm too distracted to focus. Whereas a two-hour break playing my favorite game is just what I need to recharge my battery, improve my swing, and be more efficient when I get back to work.

So any time you're dreaming of golf, but dreading the time crunch, find a nine. It's real golf. Don't let anybody tell you otherwise. ☺

n eighteen-hole golf course typically includes holes that are par-3, par-4, and even par-5. A par-3 course, however, is exactly that: Par for *every* hole is three strokes.

Which explains Reason Number One for choosing to play one: It's *way* shorter. Fewer strokes means less walking and less time needed to complete the course. An eighteen-hole par-3 takes about two and a half hours, or just over an hour if it's only nine holes. This makes par-3 courses great for beginners, seniors, and anyone short on time, patience, or endurance.

The second reason, however, is that par-3s build accuracy. Because the distance to the hole is relatively short, you can focus on hitting with precision, as opposed to power. Most beginners want to hit the ball as hard as they can (well, most men who are beginners, anyway), but as any instructor will tell you, hitting the ball as hard as you can leads to bad habits. It's far easier to improve distance, once you've got your aim down, than it is to improve accuracy once you've got the distance, especially if you've developed a hook or a slice while pounding away at the ball.

Severiano

If your ball hits a tree on its way to making par, you've hit a *Seve*. This shot pays homage to the guy who made it happen on a regular basis: the talented and tempestuous Spanish champion, Seve Ballesteros.

Annie

When you miss the fairway but still manage to make par on the hole, you've done what golf legend Arnold Palmer pulled off in many a tournament.

Precisely because par-3s emphasize precision, women excel on them. Many of us have trouble getting distance on the ball, especially in the beginning. This can become very discouraging on a regulation course, especially on those par-5 holes. If you aren't getting much distance on your ball, in fact, a par-5 hole can be downright exhausting.

Finally, par-3s are a great way to get comfortable on the gold course. Beginners rarely risk a complete round of golf; they'd rather work on their strokes at the range. But the range can get mighty boring, and then there's that temptation to bring out the driver and develop bad habits. I'm no longer a beginner, and I still favor the par-3 because it gives me the opportunity to (1) use a variety of clubs (2) in a variety of real situations (3) in half the time a full round takes. Three good reasons to put a par-3 course into your play schedule! ☺

GOLF GIRLS I ADMIRE:

Cindy Reid

She's considered the number-one female golf instructor in the world—and I'm pretty sure that if you took the word "female" out of that description, she'd still be Number One. As director of instruction at the PGA Tour's TPC Sawgrass, Cindy worked with some of the greatest (and most demanding) golfers of our time, including Vijay Singh. The finicky Fijian is not only a client but a true fan, which is evident in the foreword he wrote for her latest book, *Get Yourself in Golf Shape*.

Cindy's latest endeavor is probably her bravest ever. In 2007 she packed up her bags and headed to Shenzhen, China to open her own golf academy at Mission Hills, the world's largest golf resort with twelve top-designer championship courses. Offering both an elite school for serious golfers and a women's elite program for women who want to work on the fundamentals, Cindy believes coaching is her best shot at growing the game she loves. "As a player, the only way to succeed at the highest level is to be very self-centered," the former LPGA tournament winner notes. "Being more of a giver, I'm happiest sharing my knowledge and experience with others."

GET THE RIGHT COACH

The first thing I can tell you about choosing the right golf instructor is probably something you already know, in that intuitive way we women always know these things: Your coach should not be the man you have breakfast with in the morning. Husbands and boyfriends rarely make good golf instructors, though they frequently lobby hard for the position. It's amazing how many golf girls succumb to their partner's line of reasoning, too—forgetting, I guess, that someone with whom they've been intimate can hardly be expected to provide objective commentary on their swing.

Now that we've cleared that up, how *do* you find the best instructor? As with every important hiring, referrals are best. Ask around. Fellow golfers at your club or local course or driving range or even at work can give you some names to check out. And check them out you must: What's important isn't that you find the right coach right away, but that you take a pass on the wrong coaches immediately. That's hard for us girls, I know. We worry so much about hurting the feelings of others that we'll stay in a relationship that's not working for us way longer than we should. I suggest you be upfront: Tell each prospective coach that you're shopping around for an instructor and, to help you decide—"to see if the chemistry is right"—propose hiring the person for a session. That way, you'll feel you've been fair, and you won't feel beholden to anyone. It's important in golf, as in any relationship, to be honest about your feelings from the get-go.

You'll know, of course, when the relationship *is* right. You'll feel supported and understood. You'll feel nurtured in the approach you have and encouraged in the style you bring. You'll feel inspired to adopt suggestions, not berated into changing habits. Most important, you'll make serious progress in your game.

Bear that in mind when you break the news to your man over breakfast. ☺

IN MY FANTASY FOURSOME:

Celine Dion

Golf Le Mirage, a private club just twenty minutes outside of Montreal, features two of Quebec's most beautiful courses. Designed by Graham Cooke in the early 1990s, both the Carolina and the Arizona are known for their challenging greens, which are well fortified with sand traps, bunkers, and mounds. But the woodsy Carolina, in particular—lavishly landscaped with a profusion of blooming perennials, ornamental shrubs, and waterfalls—must have caught the discerning eye of Celine Dion, because she and her husband, René, became full owners of the club in 2000. Playing there as a guest one brisk June day, I quickly realized it was the course of my dreams. By the time I finished my round I had an all-new appreciation for Celine, whose voice has always moved me to tears.

Turns out she's quite a golfer. Apparently she practices her swing backstage and makes golf a priority pit-stop when she's touring. Celine's coach, Debbie Savoy-Morel, is now head pro at Le Mirage. But even without knowing all this, you could guess golf is a passion with her, because her touches are everywhere. I feel sure, for instance, that it was her idea to enhance Carolina's numerous shady glens with unexpected sculptures and multiple little benches. I've never played a course that offered me more rest-stops in every sense of the word (yes: bathrooms, each beautifully appointed with thoughtful toiletries). And the pro shop! Boutique Le Mirage is bright, spacious, and amply stocked, with big cushy leather chairs for spouses who might need to sit down while you contemplate all things Callaway. I came away feeling certain that whatever she shoots, Celine and I would be well matched.

GOLF TERMS FOR LOSERS

bogey finishing a hole one over par

double bogey finishing a hole two over par. This is some-times called a buzzard, probably because if you shoot it you're starting to look doomed.

triple bogey finishing a hole three over par. Anything over six strokes begins to earn more colorful terms, such as "blow-up."

snowman a score of eight, which would probably be called a "disaster" except that the figure-eight looks like a snowman.

ADDRESS THE BALL WITH YOUR DERRIÈRE

"**P**icture a railroad track," my husband urged, watching me try to position myself at the tee. "One rail is the imaginary line between your ball and your target—the marker there on the fairway, or the flag down on the green, or whatever you're shooting for. That's why it's called *the target line*. The other rail, which is parallel to the first, is the line your toes make. See?"

I didn't see. I did understand the importance of getting properly set up; that a golf swing was predicated on a combination of elements, one of them being the angle of my body as I addressed the ball. But if I kept my toes on "the rail," and didn't move my head, how was I to swivel my hips and stay on track?

Another instructor tried to get me to envision a barrel. "It's a narrow space, so you can't shift back and forth or sideways. Your backswing's gotta stay in line, and you've got to keep that line through the full swing or you'll bang up against the sides."

I nodded. It kinda made sense, on certain days. And then on others it didn't.

Only when I went back to France, and played with some of the locals, did I get advice that truly helped me grasp how to address the ball. "Bend from the hips, not your waist," one of them, a psychologist, advised. Then he leaned in and said, more quietly, "Your . . . ahem . . . derrière is going to stick out. *Ce n'est pas élégant, vraiment, mais . . .*" And he shrugged in that distinctively French way that makes you think you should maybe just lighten up a bit and see what happens. I leaned over from my hips, bent my knees slightly and, sure enough, my derrière was out there. But now I understood what this accomplished: With my weight on the balls of my feet, I could swing through without changing my alignment. The position, and the sensation, made me suddenly remember all the hours I'd spent as a girl in a ballet studio, practicing my *pliés* before a mirror at the barre. Yes! Addressing the ball had something of ballet! Stillness with movement!

Back home I took up my golf drills in front of a mirror. Now I could *really* see: Just as I wasn't supposed to stray from a section of the mirror as I *pliéd*, I wouldn't allow my body to leave its narrow section of the mirror as I practiced my swing.

It's made a big difference. I'd be willing to bet that for us girls, better positioning is the key to a better swing. Men, of course, focus on the swing itself because that's where all the action is for them, the physically forceful aspect of getting the job done. They step up to the tee, stare down the fairway, fixate on the flag, and launch right into their swing because they're *outcome-oriented*, as Judith Rosener, a professor at the University of California in Irvine, has observed. But they often don't get the outcome they're fixated on, because they don't take the time to refocus on the ball and reorient accordingly. They're not, as we are, *process-oriented* enough.

Now that I see the connection between golf and dance, I'm working on incorporating my belly dancing into my fitness routine and even into some of my golf drills. In belly dancing, as in golf, the whole idea is to isolate certain body parts and keep them motionless while revving up the action in, say, the hips. I think it could revolutionize women's golf. It's a matter of getting comfortable, as my French friend pointed out, with our derrières. ☺

DRESS TO ADDRESS

Instead of feeling insecure about the bootyful posture, I own it. I'm particularly fond of flouncy skirts with pleats, ruffles, or piping, and built-in bike shorts. I have a couple of skirts whose undergarment is in a contrasting color, or is edged in one: lavender on dark purple, pale blue on periwinkle, pink with turquoise trim. If, when I address the ball, *ce n'est pas élégant*, I guarantee that flash of contrasting color will keep everyone from noticing my less-than-perfect swing!

THAT GOES FOR YOU GUYS, TOO

Chris DeMarco is a PGA golfer who maintained a Top-Ten ranking for over fifty weeks between 2002 and 2006. In the spring of 2008, playing in Korea at the Ballentine Championship, he struggled with his driving until his wife remarked, "You used to stick your butt out like you were wearing a dress." He finished up the round with an awesome sixty-eight. After a week of hitting solid shots, he told reporters, "It's amazing, the simplicity of that advice. Sure enough, it just kind of kicked everything right into gear."

WAGGLE AWAY

One of the most evocative golf terms you'll hear—and you'll hear a lot of evocative golf terms—is "waggle." It conjures up images of Marilyn Monroe walking down a train platform in *Some Like It Hot*, or Angelina Jolie in . . . well, in everything she does. The waggle, however, has nothing to do with a slinky hip sashay (otherwise known as the "wiggle"; see below). The golfer's definition is actually quite drab: "To make small movements of the club head back and forth at approach, prior to grounding the club."

I know—*yawn*, right?

The thing is, though, the waggle has a purpose in the golf swing, a purpose that many women just don't get, and even when they do get it, hesitate to exploit. Men waggle because it helps them achieve the desired swinging tempo before they actually swing. While they're waggling, they're visualizing the swing and forming the clear intention that will get the ball to fly straight and true. Which is why you'll see men doing double waggles or triple waggles or however many waggles it takes to launch a good swing, utterly heedless of how many people are waiting to tee off behind them. They're not thinking about other golfers; they're clearing their mind of nongolf thoughts. They're finding their tempo, which is as important to golf as it is to . . . uh . . . other important things.

So now you see why almost all the guys waggle. And you can also probably see why we girls rarely do, being the more considerate and self-conscious species. We're just way too concerned about (1) not keeping our playing partners waiting, and (2) how we look, the longer we stand up there addressing the ball. Ever watch how fast women get into and out of the tee box?

But this has got to stop. To become a better golfer, you've got to waggle. You've got to get yourself a preshot routine, and the waggle can be a key component of that. Treat it as your magic wand, like the guys do. Every time you get in the box, set up, look at your target, look at the ball, waggle, visualize, waggle, silence all doubts, waggle . . . and let 'er rip. ☺

Why We Wiggle

Not to be confused with the waggle (see above), the wiggle is nonetheless a key statistic in determining a golf girl's success, both on the course and off. Measurements aren't always necessary—some golf girls obviously have plenty of wiggle. But to what *degree* could mean the difference between a birdie and a bogey.

This is where a study by British mathematicians has provided a remarkable insight. Apparently a waist circumference that is 70 percent of the hip circumference is the ratio that provides the maximum amount of wiggle in a girl's walk. The study reported that Marilyn Monroe had a ratio of 0.69—almost perfect, as if we couldn't have guessed. But here's the bit of breakthrough news: Actress Jessica Alba has *exactly* the .70 ratio, hence the perfect wiggle. And guess what? Jessica is a golfer, and a good one.

I rest my case.

LOVE THAT LEFT FOOT

Even before he spoke to me, I noticed him: tall and muscular, bronzed skin, chiseled features, Daniel Craig blue eyes. He dressed, too, as if he were heading to the Augusta National, with creased slacks, Ralph Lauren polo, and bespoke golf shoes. Usually the guy in the bay next to me at the driving range is wearing cargo shorts and a sloppy tee. Which is fine, but the contrast here was somewhat disarming.

"I hope you don't mind me saying so," he began, "but I can't help but notice you're shanking the ball big time."

Was I? A rank beginner, I was happy just to be making contact with the ball.

"One way you could fix that quickly," he continued, "would be to keep your knee straight. You're bending it when you swing, and that's lifting your left heel off the ground." He pulled back his driver and swung through, so I could see how effortlessly his lean body moved. His heel stayed rooted. "See? If you lift your heel, you're going to mishit the ball."

"Thanks," I said. And I meant it. I did need some pointers, and he seemed to know what he was talking about.

Sure enough, when I got home and looked at my videos, there it was: my unruly left foot. Immediately I set out to correct it. *Keep that knee straight!* became my new swing thought. I went back to the range, and methodically worked on keeping my heel down.

Disaster ensued.

I was playing with friends a couple weeks later, and was

playing so poorly I felt I had to offer an explanation. "It's because I'm trying to correct for my terrible habit of bending my knee and lifting my heel through the swing," I confessed. "It's just not coming easily."

My partner shook his head. "Pat," he said, leaning on his 7-iron and smiling. "That works for some people, but what makes a good golf swing isn't set in stone. It's highly individual. You might be better off doing what you do naturally."

Well, it only took a couple of holes to see that he was right. I let my left foot do what it wanted to during my swing, and by the end of the round, I was playing better.

What took longer to figure out, though, was why I'd listened to a perfect stranger and worked so hard to implement his advice. Yes, he was sexy. But mainly, because the guy had spoken with such authority, I just reflexively, almost childishly, obeyed him. Why do we women value a male opinion over our own loud and clear instinct? I was kind of disgusted with myself.

On further reflection, though, I realized *all* golfers are vulnerable to the illusion of the perfect swing—even the pros. Just consider LPGA player Natalie Gulbis, who has won the Évian Women's Open, has racked up dozens of top-ten finishes, and has been for several seasons a valued member of the U.S. Solheim Cup Team. She is famous for her unusual corkscrew swing. Watch her closely sometime, and you'll see how much more swivel and torque goes into her drive. Yet for years, she was advised to reengineer her swing. Good girl that she is, Natalie even hired top swing coach Bruce Harmon to help her make changes. But in the end she kept much of her highly criticized corkscrew, because, as it turns out, she has an extra vertebra in her back. *Wow*, right? (If I'm upset about losing a couple weeks of my recreational season to a bit of bad heel advice, think how Gulbis must feel about the months she spent on the circuit trying to overcome an extra vertebra!)

The moral of this story? Beware of those who try to "set you straight," because even though the golf swing IS the most complicated thing in any sport, it's also a whole lot more individual than we're taught. Get some proper instruction, sure. But if you get into a swing rut, trying to incorporate all the tips you've received, try doing what feels natural. Give in to instinct. In my experience, this will give you back your confidence. And that's key, not just for getting your game back, but also for reclaiming the joy of playing—which is why you're working on your swing in the first place. Just remember that the next time someone advises you on how to perfect your form.☺

SQUEEZE AND SWING

ut of a rather dry discussion on how to cure a slice came this provocative pearl from my fellow blogger, Canadian *Golf Gal*, aka Gail Moss: "Squeeze your boobies."

It's not the sort of advice you're likely to forget, especially if, like me, you already suspect your anatomy is, um, *in the way*. When I first started playing golf, I blamed every slice or shank or big whiff on my breasts. Like golf announcer Ben Wright, who infamously proclaimed that "women are handicapped by having boobs," I believed my bra size explained my lousy swing.

But when I read Golf Gal's advice, and learned that she'd gotten it from Ben Hogan, I figured it was worth a try. Sure enough, my slice was soon a thing of the past.

Now it's clear to me why. When you squeeze your breasts together, you keep your arms closer to your body, which keeps them straighter through the swing—no more "chicken wings," as so many instructors call those flailing elbows. So my breasts weren't the problem; my arms were. But "Don't flail your elbows!" isn't a good swing thought, largely because it's negative. Far better, and easier to act on, is to tell yourself what you *should* do. And that, ladies, is "Squeeze your boobies!" ☺

GOLF GIRL'S TOP FIVE

Movie Picks

1. Tin Cup I loved this movie before I ever thought of playing golf. Kevin Costner, who plays the frat-boy driving range owner, falls for Rene Russo, the new shrink in town, who comes to the range for golf lessons because she's dating Don Johnson, a golf pro. To win her heart, he decides he has to win the U.S. Open—and very nearly does (win the Open, that is). The first time I saw it, I just loved the romantic comedy aspect. I saw it again after I'd started playing golf, and the scene where he finds the water on the last hole of the Open resonated on a whole different level.

2. Pat and Mike Katharine Hepburn and Spencer Tracy? What's not to love? Katharine Hepburn is very convincing as Pat, the athlete who ends up playing golf against such real stars as Babe Didrikson Zaharias. Spencer Tracy plays Mike Conovan, her promoter—the usual tough guy. But this is one of the rare Tracy/Hepburn movies where he gives in to her in the end. Who wouldn't?

3. Caddyshack Though this 1980 farce remains a cult classic on and off the golf circuit, I must admit, I didn't like it when I saw it in my nongolfing days. Once I started playing, though, I found a lot to laugh at in Rodney Dangerfield's assault on country-club society, Bill Murray's all-out war on the gophers ruining the golf course, and Ted Knight's club-throwing tantrums during tournament play. However, I still can't quote whole scenes verbatim like many men can.

4. Babe Not the pig movie, but the 1975 made-for-TV biopic about all-round athlete and golf star Babe Didrikson Zaharias. Susan Clark won an Emmy for her portrayal of the legendary champion, and the film won a Golden Globe for Best Motion Picture Made for Television. Hard to find, but worth the effort.

5. Dead Solid Perfect It's quite common to fantasize about being a professional golfer, but this movie, based on the book by Dan Jenkins (*Semi-Tough*), shows the gritty side of the biz. Randy Quaid plays the struggling tournament golfer who tries to hustle every player he meets, including Jack Warden, who sponsors him on the tour. The ending's predictable, and the story gets a bit melodramatic at times, but Quaid—quite a good golfer in real life—makes it well worth watching.

PRACTICE LIKE A GIRL

Ever watch guys at the driving range? To a man, they're all out there . . . *driving*. Working on your golf game, if you're male, means buying the extra-large bucket of balls, bringing out Big Bertha, and whacking away as hard as you can until your thumb blisters or your back aches or your shoulder needs ice.

A better way to practice, particularly if you're new to golf, is to go to the range with your entire bag of clubs, buy the large bucket . . . and leave your driver in the bag. Instead, you're going to start swinging with your most humble tool, the one that'll give you the shortest distance: the sand wedge. After about ten balls, you'll have learned just what kind of loft and distance and drop and roll you can get from your sand wedge. Make a mental note or, better yet, jot down your findings. Next, pull out the pitching wedge: Same drill. After the wedges, it's time for the 9-iron, followed by the 7, and then the 5. Some purists might recommend you go right down to the longest iron, but I find it more instructive to substitute my round-headed hybrids at this point, because they're easier to use. Only when you've given each of these clubs ten to twelve balls should you pull out your driver, tee up the remaining balls, and send them into the ether.

The whole exercise takes twenty to thirty minutes— a bit more if you paused to note down what kind of shot each club produced.

I practice two or three times a week at the range. However, I put in an equal amount of time at our chipping/pitching area. It's a practice green about the size of a basketball court whose undulations and sand traps allow me to practice all sorts of different lies. On the putting green, I incorporate a few of these drills into my weekly routine:

(1) Take six balls and drop them in a circle around the pin about two feet out. Try to sink each two-foot putt.

(2) Develop new ways of looking at the ball. I've got a gadget that draws a line on the ball to help me visualize a straight putt. It's amazing how, after you use a marked ball for about fifteen minutes, you can "see" that line even when it's no longer there.

(3) Get your partner to hold your head down as you putt. This technique was popularized by Michelle Wie's mom, who has been observed holding down Michelle's head for *hours* lest she lift it while putting.

(4) Drop balls into the rough around the green and practice chipping and pitching them in. This kind of practice can actually be fun. And, it's often that chip onto the green that makes or breaks your score on a hole.

If my schedule allows it, I head over to our lovely little par-3 to play a practice round. When both time and weather conspire against me, I go to our golf performance center. It's got all sorts of high-tech gizmos to help me improve my game: a putting-line machine; a bionic vest you wear that tracks your every swing move and documents it on a nearby screen; simulators to give you the experience of playing, say, Spyglass at Pebble Beach or Sawgrass in Jacksonville. And in a real pinch, I've been known to work on my game in my home.

Bottom line, girls: Practice all you can, but keep it short, keep it fun, and stay with it. Practice doesn't make perfect, but it sure helps. ☺

GOLF GIRLS I ADMIRE:

Babe Didrikson Zaharias

For all-round athleticism, no golfer, male or female, has ever come close to Babe. Christened Mildred, she got her nickname as a girl after scoring five home runs in a single baseball game. At the age of twenty, she led the Golden Cyclones, her company basketball team, to victory in the American Athletic Union championship. A year later, after setting five world records in the high jump, javelin, eighty-meter hurdles, and baseball throw, she competed in the Olympics as a track-and-field star, bringing home two golds and a silver. At the relatively late age of twenty-four she picked up golf, the sport for which she would become best known.

Babe started her golf career playing against men in the PGA. With the exception of her first attempt at the Los Angeles Open, where she met her husband, professional wrestler George Zaharias, she made the cut in every PGA tournament she ever entered. As an amateur she won seventeen straight championships, something no other player in the history of the sport has ever done. After winning the 1946–47 U.S. Women's Championships, as well as the 1947 British Ladies' Championship and three Western Open victories, she turned pro, dominating what was to become, thanks to her, the LPGA. She finished her career in the late fifties with a total of eighty-two victories. There wasn't a title in golf that Babe hadn't won.

As much as I admire her for her athletic gifts, I think it's worth mentioning her fun, flirty, and fashionable side. Babe was a state-champion seamstress who designed and made most of her own golf clothes, for instance. And get this: she had a vaudeville career. A singer and harmonica player, Babe actually recorded a couple of songs. My kinda girl!

"The Babe has arrived. Now, who's coming in second?"

—Babe Didrikson Zaharias

GET HANDICAPPED

*A*t the start of my second season of golf, I began playing once a week in an Executive Women's Golf Association league. From the start I reveled in the social aspect of playing golf with a diverse group of women, and in the friendly competition that encouraged me to challenge myself. So I decided to put in a call to the ladies' league at my municipal course, the magnificent Richter Park in Danbury, Connecticut. Why not play in their league too? I'd get to play more often, I'd meet more people, and I'd be able to enjoy the hilly splendor of Richter on a weekly basis. "What steps do I have to take to sign up?" I asked the Richter league rep. There was a tiny silence. Then this terse reply: "What is your handicap?" While the EWGA does urge players to establish a handicap as soon as possible, they hadn't made it a requirement for joining them. They had signed me right up, and I was out on the course with them the next day. "Well, I don't have one yet," I admitted, sensing this was the wrong answer. "I'm just now getting registered—."

"Do you hit a hundred and fifty yards off the tee?" she interrupted. "Can you get out of a sand trap?" Now I was really flummoxed. "Look," she continued, "for your sake, and for ours, I'm going to suggest you take a few lessons and get better, because we're pretty competitive." She then proceeded to tell me about this newcomer to the league who got in a sand trap, picked up her ball, and threw it onto the green because she knew she couldn't hit it out. "We just can't have that," she concluded. "So we don't accept a handicap greater than . . . ." She hesitated. "*Twenty*."

I share this story not for what it says about the local ladies but rather to show how the golf handicap has come to be used, far too often, as an *exclusionary* qualification. Women, in particular, are intimidated by it—even women who, like my friend Erika, can hit longer and straighter than a lot of guys. "Oh, I can't play in the tournament," she balked when I suggested she participate in an annual charity event, sponsored by the local volunteer fire department. "*I don't even have a handicap.*"

How ironic, since the golf handicap was invented to *cancel out* the sort of differences that keep beginners from playing with veterans. Golf's forefathers (yes, men) perceived that the game was difficult enough that newcomers wouldn't stand a chance at learning it if left to themselves. The handicap was a way to level the playing field, a way to keep less skilled players in the company of those who had much to teach them. Skilled players could afford to welcome rank beginners to their foursome without fearing for the bottom line on the scorecard. In short, far from being a barrier, the handicap was designed to act as a lever. No other sport offers such an accommodation.

I suspect that the intimidation the handicap prompts in women—which allows it to be used as an exclusionary tactic—has a lot to do with its calculus, because *arriving* at a handicap can be pretty complicated. You've got to know stuff like course rating and slope and handicap differential, and then understand how those factors equate to something called the *handicap index*. It's the sort of technical data men can't get enough of, and will bore you to tears trying to explain. Suffice it to say, however, that you will never have to calculate your handicap by yourself. Getting handicapped is simply a matter of going to the desk at your club or course, asking to be registered, and submitting your scores. Once you've submitted at least three rounds (some desks will insist on five), you'll be issued a USGA handicap. As you keep submitting rounds, the desk staff will keep crunching the numbers to update your handicap. It's a great way to chart your own progress.

And the ladies at Richter notwithstanding, it's also a great way to get yourself more game. Once I had a handicap, I found myself being welcomed into more games—notably, the ones that included betting. I can't tell you how much fun it is to play a hole and win five bucks simply because my handicap allowed me ten strokes to their five!

There is one *good* reason why women put off getting handicapped: We're just not all that obsessed with keeping score, certainly not the way guys are. My husband would *never* say, as my girlfriends and I often do, "Oh, I'm just going to work on my shot-making"; you should see the look of total consternation when I tell him not to put me down for anything. Even when I set out scoring a round, if I blow up on a couple of holes I quit keeping score, because I just don't see the point. I'm a firm believer in having fun, and scoring, when you're just starting out, can take the fun right out of the game.

But don't put off forever getting handicapped. I'm glad I didn't wait beyond my second season. My index was 32 when I first registered, and now I'm down to 24. These days I occasionally break 100 on a round, which means I'm closing in on that magical handicap of 20. *That* will be a huge victory for me, whether or not it satisfies the requirements of the Richter Ladies' League! ☺

IN MY FANTASY FOURSOME:

John Updike

[O]nce in a while a 7-iron rips off the clubface with that pleasant tearing sound, as if pulling a zipper in space, and falls toward the hole like a raindrop down a well; or a drive draws sweetly with the bend of the fairway and disappears, still rolling, far beyond the applauding sprinkler; these things happen in spite of me, and not because of me, and in that sense I am free, on the golf course, as nowhere else.
—John Updike, *Golf Dreams*

Golf Dreams is the best golf writing I've ever read; it may be, in fact, just the best writing I've ever read. Updike's collection of essays, poems, and short fiction reveals such a heartfelt passion for the game that you feel you haven't really lived if you don't get out there on the course and see what he's talking about. There's no sound, no feel, no smell, no scene he cannot capture; you can almost taste the air on that balmy coastal course he describes, almost hear the crunch of grass on the frost-stiffened fairways he plays. And with every keen observation he makes, you get a dose of his self-effacing humor. After reading *Golf Dreams*—in one intense sitting—I couldn't help but fantasize about playing a round with the master wordsmith. What a huge pity he is gone—gone to those Elysian fairways in the Great Beyond. But I'll bet his handicap has gone to zero.

PLAY GAMES

Instead of playing golf, many golfers play golf games, most of which involve . . . betting.

Betting is not illegal in golf. In a 2006 survey that *Golf Digest* conducted online, 93 percent of respondents admitted to betting at least occasionally. Having a bit of money riding on an outcome certainly spices things up, especially if you've been playing for decades. And shifting the focus from winning a round to winning a hole makes golf more attractive to those who are less skilled or just starting out. I'm a big proponent of not keeping score in favor of keeping the game fun, and golf games are a great way to do that.

Bingo Bango Bongo

Rather than keep score in this game, you award yourself points. Point values are as follows:

> First ball on the green = 1 point
> Closest ball to the pin = 1 point
> First putt to sink = 1 point

Needless to say, each point carries a cash value (whatever you and your partners assign it). One variation is to double the points for any player who wins all three of the possible points on a hole. I love this game because, while I rarely win a round by shooting the lowest score, I stand a fighting chance of winning based on sheer point accumulation.

Nassau

The Nassau divides up an eighteen-hole course into three betting opportunities: the front nine, the back nine, and the full eighteen. The lowest score for each sector wins the bet, which is usually five dollars.

One Club

As the name implies, you must choose and use only one club to get you through the entire round, with the exception of the greens (where the putter is used instead). It's a great way to develop your expertise in the use of that particular club. I credit my expertise with the 7-iron to this game.

Pink Lady

An eighteen-hole round gets apportioned into three six-hole games. Every player but one uses a white ball; one player starts off shooting a low-compression pink ball. The idea is to neither lose the pink ball nor wind up with it at the end of each six-hole game. On the first

garbage

Placing bets in golf is not only legal, it's a great way to add fun to the game. And because there are endless opportunities to make a wager, *garbage* is the term used to encompass all the idiosyncratic ones. At the beginning of a round, players will assign point values to, say, the longest drive off the tee, or making birdie (one stroke under par) on a particular hole, or number of balls lost. All such miscellaneous bets fall under the umbrella of *garbage*.

hole, the player with the highest score becomes "the pink lady," or the one who has to play the pink ball on the next hole. (In the case of a tie for highest score, the two players have to compete in a tiebreaker.) The player who emerges from a six-hole round without the pink ball earns a point. The player who manages to play a hole under par earns three points. The player who loses the pink ball awards each of the other players with a three-point bonus. I've learned that merely having the "toxic" pink ball makes me hit it into water hazards. Still, like musical chairs, Pink Lady rewards you for being not the best, but for not being the worst.

Round Robin

An eighteen-hole round gets divided into three "matches" of six holes. Before each match, players rotate partners so that, by the end of the round, each player has managed to play with each of her partners. The objective is to win the most six-hole matches. I find it's a good way to get to know the members of a foursome. You won't always like everybody, of course, but diplomacy gets rewarded: The better you play with everyone, the more likely you'll win all three rounds.

Sandies

The wager here is that you'll manage to get yourself out of a sand trap or bunker and onto the green in one stroke. Personally, I rarely play this, because I can't even get out, let alone in one stroke. A golfer automatically wins the bet if, instead of getting out in a stroke, she manages to win the hole on or under par.

Scramble

This isn't so much a game as a very popular way to play the game of golf, because beginners aren't at all disadvantaged by their lack of skills. Here's how it works: Everyone hits off the tee, but then everybody brings their ball and drops it a club-length away from where the best ball has landed. Play proceeds in this way until everyone's on the green, where you hit your own putts. Not only does the game really move along, but no one suffers from poor technique or excessive frustration.

Skins

Each hole is assigned a set value, or skin. No one knows why, exactly, this term came into use, but one explanation is that when furriers would arrive in Scotland from distant lands they would gamble their pelts, or skins, on golf. Anyway, the idea is for each player to rack up the skins by winning hole after hole. If there's a tie, nobody wins that hole; the skin value just gets added to the next hole. Over eighteen holes, a couple of ties build up quite a skin value, adding considerably to the excitement. I've also played where the skin value increases progressively as you proceed through the course. Either way, it's a lot of fun.

Shoot Out

A type of tournament format, Shoot Out begins with a field of nineteen players. On every hole, the highest-scoring player is eliminated until only one remains: the champion, crowned on the eighteenth hole. It's ultraslow, especially at the beginning, because all players play the hole, and there are usually quite a few playoffs, too. But it's lots of fun if you have a good group and plenty of time.

Snakes

In this putting game, someone gets "bitten": whoever has most recently three-putted. At the beginning of the round, all players in the foursome agree on an amount the loser will pay to the

to sandbag, or be a sandbagger

No discussion of golf handicaps can be complete without referencing the *sandbagger*, someone who deliberately misleads others about her ability level, claiming to be worse than she actually is in order to better her chances of winning.

Sandbaggers artificially inflate their handicap by submitting only their worst rounds of golf for handicapping. They'll enter a tournament with, for example, a handicap index of 18 when, in fact, their true handicap might be closer to 12. *Voila!* They've just bought themselves a deduction of six extra strokes off their gross score, improving their chances of winning the tournament. This is otherwise called *hustling.*

Sandbaggers aren't unique to golf. Just about every competitive sport where bets are made has its cheaters, hustlers, and sandbaggers. Gang members, it turns out, ambushed their rivals with actual sandbags—not fifty-pound burlap sacks, but socks filled with sand—which is how the term crept into sports.

It took a while for it to find its way into golf circles, however. According to Word-Detective.com, it was by way of poker that sandbagging began to describe a player who misrepresents his ability to gain an advantage. This makes a lot of sense, given that poker is about betting and little else. The poker sandbagger would, upon being dealt a fantastic hand, delay upping the ante in order to lull the other players into a false sense of security. Only when the stakes were sufficiently high would the sandbagger pounce, "clobbering the other players with his good hand."

other players. Play proceeds from hole to hole, and whoever three-putts gets and keeps the "snake" until someone else three-putts. Whoever is the last to be holding the snake pays the other players in the foursome the agreed amount. When my foursome plays, we bring along the rubber snake that decorates our house at Halloween for authenticity.

Splashies

A splashie is a side bet, one based on how players handle hitting the water. If a player achieves par on a hole, despite hitting into water, he wins a "splashie." The value of the watery win is agreed upon before the round begins.

MAKE GREAT ESCAPES

've been in sand pits so deep you need a ladder to get out. This is tough on the psyche. Here's what I've learned about handling those infamous bunker shots:

1. Hunker down. Knees should be flexed, shoulders forward, waist bent.

2. Lift the ball with your club as though it were a champagne glass. You're trying to swing as flat along the ground as you can. But be careful with your practice swing: A player may not touch sand in a bunker with her club. If you do, it'll cost you two strokes.

3. Take a sand-trap tutorial. Lots of courses and ranges offer them. It's basically an afternoon in the bunkers with a bunch of other frustrated golfers. But you'll get to work on all sorts of lies, and by watching others you'll pick up on what works and what doesn't. This will boost your confidence, which is half the battle.

4. Practice getting out of a trap at every noncompetitive opportunity. If I'm playing in a tournament, I'm not going to waste precious strokes hacking away at my ball. But otherwise, I try to do just that.

5. Try a sand wedge with bigger loft. I like the fifty-six–degree wedge more than the sixty. Both my husband and I love the Easy

Out golf wedge because it's darn near horizontal.

6. Beware the fried egg. You know, when the ball has plopped down into a ring of sand like a sunny-side-up yolk. I've been told the only way to handle this notoriously difficult shot is to hit the ball by hitting the sand behind it. The idea is to send the sand, and incidentally the ball with it, out of the trap. But this has never actually worked for me. Instead, I tend to hit a chip shot, the same technique I'd use on the rough. Instead of carving a divot, I bring up a fistful of sand. It's probably time I take the sand-trap course at my local driving range.

7. Make a game of it. Agree at the outset that for every bunker shot, you get specially rewarded for getting out. That way you're less likely to go rigid with anxiety every time your playing partners shriek, "Oh my GOSH! You're in the BEACH!"

8. Strategize to avoid the trap in the first place. Sand is invariably placed to penalize those who overestimate their abilities. This tends to be men who, when confronted with a dogleg in the fairway at 150 yards, assume they'll be able to drive their way over it. Women, in contrast, see two 150-yard segments and know they'll be better off laying up, or taking two drives to get to the green.

9. "Pot" bunkers that require an unsteady wooden ladder to reach your ball are scary on so many levels. Best to avoid these courses altogether . . . unless you've taken the sand-trap course.

10. Pick up your ball, chuck it onto the green, and take the one-stroke penalty. ☺

GOLF GIRLS I ADMIRE:

Alice Dye

We're used to hearing about Pete Dye, the architect renowned for devilish and distinctive courses all over the world. But Alice Dye is a designer in her own right, an author, and a winner of more than fifty amateur golf titles, including two nationals. One of golf's biggest promoters, she is perhaps best known for her input on the most recognized and most difficult holes in all of golf: the TPC Sawgrass seventeenth. In 1980, during construction of the Stadium Course at TPC Sawgrass in Ponte Vedra Beach, Florida, she listened to hubby Pete debate what to do about the seventeenth hole, whose sand had been mined out completely and dispersed to other areas of the course. Upon viewing the huge hole, Alice suggested it be excavated even further to create an "island green" surrounded by water. As Alice wrote in her 2004 book, *From Birdies to Bunkers*, grounds crews recover some 200,000 balls from the water around the island each year. In one round of the PGA's Players Championship in 2007, a record fifty balls ended up in the pond.

I don't know that I need to play *that* particular course, but I am dying to try the Pound Ridge Golf Club, a championship public course in New York's Westchester County, which octogenarians Alice and Pete recently completed. Maybe she'd join me for a round and give me the inside scoop on every hole, because I suspect I would need all the help I can get.

PLAY BY THE RULES (NO GIMMIES!)

my first season of golf was played exclusively with men. I'd go out with my husband and each week his various friends would join us to complete the foursome. Our games would generally be quite competitive, too, often ending with an animated analysis of the scorecard. So I learned how to move through the course and keep score . . . from men.

Needless to say, I was in for quite a surprise when, the following year, I joined a ladies' league and began playing with women. Because I learned that we girls adhere to a decidedly higher standard of play.

From the first tee playing with my female foursome, I noticed the difference. As relative strangers to each other, we reviewed the basic rules we'd be playing by (unheard of among the men I play with), agreeing that we'd give ourselves "one mulligan per nine holes." Just like that, it was established—and it was adhered to throughout the game. No one took more than her allotted two mulligans, no matter what kind of trouble she found herself in. In contrast, during my games with the guys, "do-overs" were commonplace and generally not counted in the final scores because *you guys know I don't hit like that* or *I just don't want to hold everyone up looking for my ball.* No wonder men's scores are so much lower: They don't count the bad strokes!

On the green, the women I played with holed every putt— even when three or (shudder) four putts were required. They didn't waste time anguishing over their putts, either, as men often claim: They just hit them in. Men, on the other hand, rarely bother with a

billigan

A do-over, especially in the company of former president Clinton. Otherwise known as a mulligan, or any retake that doesn't get recorded as a penalty stroke on the scorecard.

putt that's less than "a few feet." They have those short putts down, so what's the point? They don't want to slow everyone down.

In short, guys don't play by the rules—not in golf and, I'm sure you've noticed, not in business or in relationships, either.

How to cope? Nina DiSesa, chairman and CEO of McCann Erickson Global, the world's largest advertising network, insists women need to accept that, on the course and off, it's not a level playing field—and then move on. "Get over it," she writes in her book, *Seducing the Boys Club*. "Then go figure out your game plan for playing ball with the big boys."

Nina's own game plan is S&M (that's seduction & manipulation) and it certainly has relevance for golf girls. She emphasizes using certain tried-and-true female tactics—flirting, flattery, and gentle persuasion—to diffuse animosity and encourage openness in situations that have the potential to become adversarial.

Personally I've found this to be precisely the tactic to deploy when meeting up with, say, a foursome of male curmudgeons on the second tee. In such situations I've noticed that a smile and a compliment go a long way toward lightening any latent tension. Friendliness, which may well come off as flirtiness, has the added benefit of nipping in the bud any brewing you're-playing-too-slow animosity. So by being true to my female tendencies, I can reprogram (okay, manipulate) the way the curmudgeons perceive me. Then I can relax and play like a girl—by the rules, that is.

And honestly, why should we golf girls feel defensive or be apologetic about the way *we* play? I know that the fewer mulligans I take, and the more putts I finish off, the better golfer I'm going to become, and the more I'm going to enjoy playing. Isn't that what it's all about? Guys, with their do-overs and gimmes, are just cheating themselves. ☺

On the Origin of Billigans

In Arkansas for a children's golf clinic, Tiger Woods was asked about playing golf with former president Bill Clinton. The two had played a round before the opening of the Tiger Woods Learning Center in Anaheim, California.

Woods described a hole on the back nine. "President Clinton rolls one in the bushes, then hits another one off the tee. Right in the middle of the fairway, he hits a nice little wedge shot. Lands onto the green maybe six or seven feet from the cup.

"Well, I hit a bad pitch. I blasted it by about twelve feet. I'm crouching down when all of a sudden I see President Clinton do one of these"—Woods bends over and plucks an imaginary ball from the turf.

"I mean, it was six or seven feet! And he pocketed it and walked off the green! So I finish up and head back to the cart, where President Clinton's sitting, writing down the numbers. I happen to kind of . . ."—Woods leaned back as if reading a scorecard over someone's shoulder—"and see: Woods four, Clinton *three*.

"Interesting math," Woods concluded, drawing a knowing laugh from his fans.

HOW TO PLAY LIKE A CELEBRITY

Use a foot wedge. This little device is an ingenious way of getting your ball out of the rough or moving it up into a more favorable spot on the green or fairway. After checking your surroundings and making sure nobody's watching, slide the wedge onto the instep of your shoe. Position yourself discreetly and perform a soccer-style kick to the ball. Remove the foot wedge, put it in your pocket, and proceed without penalty.

Put yourself down for fewer strokes. While an offense worthy of immediate disqualification on the tour, marking down your scorecard is by far the most effective way to win. Either amend your score, if someone else wrote it down, or exercise some poor math skills to come up with a tally that beats your opponents. But don't be greedy. If you subtract too many shots from your score, your opponent—who has, after all, watched how you actually play—may well suspect you of more than poor math skills.

Constantly distract your opponent. An explosive cough or yelp during his or her backswing is the time-honored method, but there are other, more subtle ways. For example, move around in your opponent's periphery. Your restlessness should be enough to interrupt his or her swing thoughts. Similarly, stand at the cup when opponents are putting and, just as they pull back for the stroke, walk toward them. This screws up their depth perception.

Pretend to keep up. Golf can be a game of endurance. There's the drink or two at lunch, and then the beer-sipping between holes, and rarely a bathroom to relieve the mounting pressure. Best not to indulge, or at least not at the same pace as your opponents. Sober players retain a clear and substantial advantage.

IN MY FANTASY FOURSOME:

Jack Nicholson

In *About Schmidt*, my favorite film ever, Jack Nicholson plays a retired widower in search of his own relevance. He hides nothing and holds nothing back, proving himself fearless—and that's just one of the reasons I'd love to play golf with him. Another is the fact that he took up the game at age fifty-two, just because he wanted a sport he could get better at as he aged. Jack never plays for money. He's notoriously relaxed about tee times (three p.m. is his preference) and rules (multiple mulligans are just fine), which says to me he plays for the pure pleasure of the game. And finally, Jack is known for genuinely encouraging his playing partners—not what you'd expect from the Joker. If he thinks you deserve a better score, he'll shave a few strokes off your round. And if he thinks he deserves a better score, well—he'll give himself one.

"It's pretty much a breeze to shoot in the eighties—you just stay out of the water and the woods. Which I can do, partly because I'll kick it out of the woods."

—Jack Nicholson, the *Golf Digest* interview, December 2007

WIN BY THE RULES (NO CHEATING!)

"There's that old saying that if you're not cheating, you're not trying," Meg Mallon, the four-time LPGA championship winner, once said. "Maybe in other sports that's true, but not in golf."

Meg should know. One year at the LPGA event in Toledo, Ohio, she was leading the tournament through one round. But in the second round, her ball hung on the lip of the cup, vacillating. She waited . . . and the ball dropped in.

Not until after she signed her scorecard did she get to wondering if she'd perhaps waited too long. In golf there's something called the ten-second rule, which states that any player who waits more than ten seconds to play a ball hovering on the edge of the cup should be assessed a penalty. So the next morning, Meg consulted a rules official. Together they watched a video of the incident, and to Meg's horror, nineteen seconds had passed. She should have assessed herself a one-stroke penalty. Worse, she had signed an incorrect scorecard. And when players sign for a score that is lower than what they actually shot, they're disqualified.

"So as the leaders are headed out to the course, my name's coming off the leader board," she recalled, grimacing at the memory.

In golf, the rulebook is sacrosanct. Each player is charged with enforcing the rules, even at great personal expense, and even (especially) when no one would be the wiser. Meg told me of another instance where she dropped her golf ball on her coin, which was used as a marker—a one-stroke penalty. "Nobody saw it," she noted, "but I couldn't play feeling I'd cheated. You just can't live with yourself if you don't call it."

There are those (see below) who don't feel this way, of course. They're notorious for cheating and, may I point out, they're *all men*. We golf girls—we play by the rules. In golf, if not in life, it's bound to get us to the winner's circle. ☺

The Social Game

REVEL IN YOUR FEMININITY

FOR DECADES, WOMEN HESITATED to be the fairer sex on the fairways. Maybe they didn't want to stand out, being the interlopers on male turf. Maybe they felt they had to prove their athleticism, lest they be dismissed for being "lesser" players. Maybe they just didn't want to garner attention for anything but their golf skills.

Whatever the reason, female golfers who suppressed their sex inadvertently perpetuated the atmosphere of all-maleness that oppressed them.

But that's changed—or at least, it's changing, and fast. Golf girls are dressing provocatively, flirting unapologetically, and socializing like . . . well, like the highly social creatures they are. And men, not surprisingly, are loving it.

I don't know why we waited so long, because golf is intrinsically social—from partners and foursomes to betting games and nineteenth holes, from nine-and-dines to member-guests. There's no better setting than a golf course to swing with an eminently eligible bachelor, if you're looking for one; if you're not, there's no greater opportunity to connect with your spouse. Most important, there's no easier way to meet new people, and kindred spirits of both sexes, than by sharing a mutual attraction to golf.

So do your part. Get out there and flaunt your femininity. Indulge your passion for fashion. Be bodacious and flirtatious, athletic and intelligent. Find fun, or make it, both on and off the course. This section will show you how.

SEX IT UP

*J*an Stephenson, winner of three majors, and one of Australia's greatest golfers ever, has no illusions about her male fans. Despite her wins and her extraordinary golf skills, she is best known for her 1980s "bubble bath" photo. In it she's relaxing in an old-fashioned, claw-footed tub brimming with golf balls. Needless to say, she's wearing nothing but the strategically placed golf balls.

Instead of lamenting that kind of notoriety as demeaning, Jan acknowledges that golf is an overwhelmingly male sport watched overwhelmingly by men (current stats put the figure at 70 percent). Since men are overwhelmingly "visual," in terms of what gets and keeps their attention, she encourages Australia's up-and-coming young golf stars to play up their looks and personalities—for the good of *women's* golf.

If you're scratching your head over this, here's her logic: Ultimately, getting women golfers noticed—never mind how—is going to send a message to women, as well as men, that women are out there on the fairways in droves. With more women playing, more women will be watching, and more women will be buying tickets, and more women will take up the sport and buy gear and watch golf. When that happens, the current (male) overemphasis on sex appeal will fade of its own irrelevance.

It's admittedly a long-term strategy. But I'm all for it, because it embraces certain realities. Men *are* visual. Women *do* like to feel attractive. And we all like to play golf well . . . and get noticed.

So you won't see me boycotting golf.com's Sexiest Women Golfers or shunning Natalie Gulbis's swimsuit calendar (I may very well launch one of my own). Why apologize for or hide assets that will lever open the club doors for all of us? ☺

GOLF GIRLS I ADMIRE:

Cristie Kerr

Mention Cristie Kerr in golf circles, and you'll hear that she's one of the game's longest drivers, most consistent putters, and strongest finishers. Twelve LPGA tournament wins and (as of this writing) the No. 1 spot on the LPGA Official Money List, Top Ten Finishes, and Rounds Under Par certainly attest to her greatness. But back in the late 1990s, soon after Cristie had turned pro, the discussion wasn't about her golf; it was about her weight. The five-foot-four golfer bordered on obesity, pushing 185 at one point. Plagued with back spasms and other physical ailments, Cristie began in earnest to diet and exercise. By 2002, she'd lost fifty pounds—and started winning tournaments. She also dropped her dowdy image, exchanging her eyeglasses for contacts, her mousy perm for sleek blond tresses, her formless bulk for a sexy svelteness. Stunning both on and off the course, Cristie is a model advocate for the benefits of methodical exercise, strict diet, and true grit.

And one more thing: In addition to working her way up the LPGA ranking ladder, Cristie brings her formidable dedication to curing breast cancer, which her mother, a diabetic and heart-attack survivor, was diagnosed with in 2003. Birdies for Breast Cancer, the foundation Cristie launched in response, has raised over $250,000 for research—an accomplishment that prompted the Susan G. Komen Breast Cancer Foundation to honor Cristie in 2006 with its LPGA Komen Award. My hat's off to this hard-working golf girl.

DON'T ACT YOUR AGE

Tiger Woods started playing golf at age two, Cristie Kerr was in competitions by the time she was seven, and by age ten Michelle Wie was consistently hitting her drives over 200 yards. They all became champions.

From this you might conclude that, to play well, you've got to start early.

But you'd be wrong. Check out *Golf Digest*'s annual Top 100 list of Hollywood golfers, and you'll see a much more interesting pattern: Champion golfers (not pro, but raising a ton of money for charity) with single-digit handicaps such as Samuel Jackson (a 4.9 handicap) and Hugh Grant (a 7) took up the sport well into adulthood. Jackson, for example, was nearly fifty when he started playing; Grant was in his late thirties; and top-ranked Dennis Quaid (a 1.1 handicap) started playing in his mid-thirties. Golf babe Téa Leoni (a 12-handicapper) got hooked at thirty-one, and Cheryl Ladd, who maintains a 14 handicap in her late fifties, began at age thirty-three.

You can learn golf at any age, and, as Jack Nicholson demonstrates, actually get better as you grow older (Jack, who took up the sport at age fifty-two, has a 12.2 handicap twenty years later). That's one of the things that make golf so appealing. The other? The handicap system means that even if you're a rank beginner at age fifty-two, you can go out and play in a foursome with Dennis Quaid without apology.

I took up golf at the advanced age of . . . well . . . let's just say I was over thirty-five. At the beginning, when I was relegated to hitting buckets of balls at the range, I worried that I had started too late. *Maybe I just don't have enough muscle memory (or flexibility, or upper body strength) to ever really get good at this*, I'd think to myself. And then, in exasperation: *Either I get good soon or put myself out to pasture*. But one day, covertly watching one of the instructors in the bay next to me, I noted his student was a woman in her late fifties. The instructor checked her stance and grip, adjusted her hands, and said something I couldn't quite hear. The woman lifted her shoulders a bit and straightened her elbows. *A late-starting newbie like me*, I thought dismissively, and bent my head to my own mat. But at that moment she unleashed a drive that made me look up: 175 yards! This was no fluke, either. Again and again, she launched the ball long and straight. Later, I asked the instructor about her. "Oh, you mean Audrey," he said, smiling. "Would you believe she picked up a club for the first time just a year ago?"

Since then, I've become a believer. Golf is a gerontologist's dream: the physical flexibility, the upper-body toning, the social interaction, the mental stimulation—it's got everything you need to keep you sharp and upright. "You're counting strokes, planning the next shot, being strategic," notes Dr. Laurel Coleman, a geriatrician from Augusta, Maine. She's on the board of the Alzheimer's Association and has an 11 handicap.

In my own golf group we have a couple of octogenarians, and at least one of them shows up when I send out an e-mail with tee times for the week. With fourteen of us in the group, some of us manage to play three times a week. We play for nickels and dimes so we can all remain friends. We often joke that "we live to play golf," but I think, in fact, by playing golf we're extending our lives.

That's my prescription, girls: Take up golf now—no age being too old—and you'll stay younger, longer. ☺

"I have to keep up with the younger players
or else they'll say,
'I have to play with that old lady.'"

—Elsie McLean, 101-year-old golfer

"I'm not just sitting around waiting for
the angel of death.
I figure he can't hit a moving target."

—Maggie Sunal, 94-year-old golfer

SHOOTING YOUR AGE

An "age shooter" is a golfer whose score matches or beats his age. For example, if Dennis Hopper shoots 91 with a handicap of 18, he scores 73—which happens to be his age.

There aren't any female age-shooters on the record books yet, but that should change as the current crop of professionals moves into middle age. Here are the numbers they'll be trying to beat:

- Youngest golfer to shoot his age: Bob Hamilton, a golf pro who scored 59 at Hamilton Golf Club in Evansville, Indiana, in 1975.

- Youngest golfer to shoot his age on the pro tour: Walter Morgan, playing the Champions Tour. In 2002, at age sixty-one, Morgan shot a 60 in the AT&T Canada Senior Open Championship.

- Youngest golfer to shoot his age on the PGA Tour: Sam "Slammin'" Snead, who fired a 67 at the Quad Cities Open in 1979, when he was sixty-seven years old. A day later, he set a new record: 66.

- Oldest golfer to shoot his age: 103-year-old Arthur Thompson of Victoria, British Columbia. Thompson was playing the Uplands Golf Club in Victoria when he accomplished the feat in 1972.

- Greatest age-shooter ever: T. Edison Smith of Moorhead, Minnesota. Frank Bailey of Abilene, Texas, had long held this record, matching or beating his age 2,623 times, from age seventy-one until age ninety-eight. But in 2006, Smith passed Bailey and continues on with the record.

SWING WITH SINGLES

Long Island Singles Speed Golf, our outrageous twist on speed dating. Men rotate from driving range station to driving range station after hitting a bucket of balls with a woman. Professional instruction provided. Scorecard matching and results sent the same night. Ages 30s-40s.

—Personal advertisement on craigslist.com

If you're a single girl, golf is the perfect medium for meeting men. The very same odds that make it difficult for women to venture out on a golf course—three out of four players are men—make it easy for women to find eminently eligible bachelors. Think about it: Your average golfer is likely to be . . .

Better Dressed – Make all the fun you want of certain golf attire. Most of it is way more stylish than men's typical attire (the cargo shorts below the knee, the shapeless tee, the sloppy running shoes). Lots of guys dress for golf, and some of the best clothing for men is designed for golf. If you doubt me, try dating bowlers, or basketball players.

Physically Fitter – I'm not saying all golfers are in good shape, but if you look at the guys playing today you'll see how athletic a bunch they've become. I credit Tiger for raising the standard (even John Daly, once the poster boy for overweight golfers, has gotten into stellar shape). With younger men in the game, there's more emphasis than ever on trim waists and broad shoulders.

Well Heeled – Golfers have money, because golf is expensive. Looking for men on a golf course means you automatically avoid slackers, misers, and the unemployed. I know I sound old-fashioned, but I think it's nice when your date can pick up the tab at the clubhouse.

Socially Adept – Golfers have nice manners. I don't know if they're better bred or they're just abiding by course etiquette, but for a fact, they're more courteous and courtly. This is especially welcome in an environment where the competition and testosterone can rise to toxic levels.

More Masculine – Did I mention the competition and testosterone?

All of this makes me wonder why any single girl would waste her time trawling match.com or eHarmony when she could get out there on the course, take her pick from a premium crop, and have a great time in the process. And guys on the course are out there for the picking, if the comments I see posted on my blog are any indication: They *want* women to see how far they can drive, how powerfully they can swing, how competently they can putt! Women, wake *up*!

In closing let me just point out that Sean Connery met his wife, Micheline, on the golf course. Now *that* makes me wish I'd taken up golf back when I was single. ☺

FINDING A (GOLF) PARTNER ONLINE

golfmates.com
The site's tag line is *Golf: The Perfect First Date*. Who could argue with that? The fact that a number of Golf Mates dates have led to commitment (to the game, and to each other) speaks well for its methodology. One Golf Mates marriage was recently featured on USA TV.

golfdates.com
The Perfect Game for Singles, Golf Dates claims—and I'd have to agree. What I'd be drawn to on this site, if I were single, would be the Dating Games, which allow you to send a "virtual smooch" or a "romantic S.O.S." There's also a Love Note Generator, a kind of digital Mad Lib that's surely a whole lot more fun than filling out eHarmony surveys.

dateagolfer.com
DateAGolfer promises to "expand your golf network," mostly by posting "looking for" classifieds. No doubt this is one way to find more partners for foursomes.

igolf.to/

Though clearly a dating site, iGolf also offers the option of connecting to other golfers for just . . . golf. Thus instead of seeking "male" or "female," iGolf lets you select "both." A big selling point here is that its partnering service is totally free. I met three of my regular golf partners through this site.

matchmaker.com
mingle2.com

These are generalized dating sites that offer golf as a defining subset. First you join, then you specify golf as a search term, and everyone posting will have a passion for golf.

EMBRACE CADDY CANDY

ack in April 2006, an enterprising golfer named Michael Trahan launched a caddy-finding service on the Web called caddychicks.com. As you can probably imagine, what you find, when you join, is not just someone to carry around your bag wherever you plan to be playing: These are young women whose primary qualification for accompanying you is that they'll look good doing it. Trahan says he got the idea after a couple of girls from Hooters followed him around during a golf tournament. Although they knew nothing about golf, Trahan insists they helped his game a lot.

I'm sure they did.

Anyway, this sparked something of a trend in unique golf services. There's now eyecandycaddies.com, whose associates are not professional caddies but, we're assured, have been trained in etiquette and safety and will provide "the best possible service."

These aren't escort or dating services. But you can understand how there might be that confusion.

How should we golf girls feel about this? I put the question to my blog readers and, predictably, the men argued that more girls on the course can only bode well for women taking up golf, while the women wondered if this sort of "entrepreneurship" is good for growing the sport or for . . . something else entirely.

I wasn't sure how I felt myself until, at our very own golf club, I started hearing about Amy, the beverage cart girl. Amy's perky blond looks and ultrashort shorts had garnered a lot of attention.

Everyone in our weekly couples' nine-and-dine was buzzing about this girl. "What a looker that Amy is!" one of the guys would say, to which another guy would respond, "And how about those outfits she wears?" There'd be a terse silence among the women, until one of the more conservative gals would insist Amy's outfits "were in clear violation of the club dress code."

Then, abruptly, the Amy conversation stopped. "Oh, she was let go," one of the wives confided. "*Too risqué.*"

Really? Was it the *shorts*? Were we golf girls *that* mean?

Finally I got the straight scoop: Amy was just not doing her job. She had no grasp of etiquette, golf or otherwise. She talked endlessly on her cell phone when she should have been attentive to her customers. As pretty as she was, she just couldn't offer "the best possible service," especially to women, whom she perceived as low tippers.

Phew. Because I think there's a place for young beautiful caddies, cart girls and golf event entertainers. They can make golf lots more fun.

Recently I came across Play Golf Designs, the brainchild of Nisha Sadekar, who played golf collegiately at the University of Missouri and professionally on the Futures Tour. Like caddychicks and eyecandy caddies, these girls are pretty, fun and flirty and some of the outfits they wear on their website would be too racy for the golf purists. But unlike the competition, Nisha's girls are elite players from all over the world and include members of the LPGA, Ladies European Tour and Duramed Futures Tour.

They enhance coporate golf events and charity tournaments with on-course contests, skills challenges and unique fundraising activities. They have a passion for the game that's reflected in the way they play and the way they manage their events.

That's the standard we should be holding these girls to, if we want to grow the sport for women. No need to punish the guys; girls who are fun, flirty, fashionable, *and* competent are exactly who we want out there on the course. ☺

PLAY WITH YOUR MAN

If you sleep with a guy, is it ever really a good idea to play golf with him?

Sitting in the clubhouse cafe after our couples' round of nine holes, I put this question out to the wives.

"Categorically no," blurted Helen, putting down her cosmopolitan.

Jennifer smiled. "It never works," she lamented, "because men are genetically programmed to give you *constant* advice."

"You're absolutely right," agreed Maggie, taking a rather large swallow of chardonnay. "It's a male thing, and it really comes out on the golf course." Maggie tipped her head in the direction of the men's table. "You saw Josh out there this evening, didn't you?"

Oh, yes. We'd all seen him. My husband, Nick, and I were the other half of his foursome, so we couldn't help but notice his cynical gaze, continually fixed on his wife, and couldn't help but hear his litany of authoritarian critiques and untimely tips. It was irksome, to say the least. But that was Josh—an extreme case, in my opinion. So I said as much. "Not every guy is that obnoxious," I pointed out.

"Of course they are!" a chorus of voices retorted. Maggie shook her head, as if it were plain as day that intimate partners couldn't afford to be golf partners.

Golf with *my* husband, while not the same as a competitive round with my girlfriends, can be just as much fun. Yes, he dispenses too much advice, but most of the time I can and do simply ignore it. Occasionally, I even learn from it. So why is playing golf with their husbands "categorically" *not* fun for these other women? Or more to the point: How could more women find joy in playing with their mates?

To get answers, I needed to cast a wider net than my circle of golf couples. So I checked with Jennifer and Greg Underwood, a couple I got to know through an online golf forum. These two run a golf shop together and play regularly in mixed competitions. They also write and edit their club's newsletter which features golf tips and advice, along with the latest scores and announcements. The monthly missives are also filled with their own personal anecdotes and opinions, which is what makes them so much fun to read. At times they disagree with each other so vehemently you have to wonder how they make their relationship work on the golf course. "Do you think husbands and wives should play golf with each other?" I asked Jennifer, who'd graciously invited me to her home for some golf-girl talk. "And if so, what's the secret to keeping it fun?"

"Greg really had to coax me to play golf, let alone play golf with *him*," Jennifer revealed, handing me a photo of herself on a Harley-Davidson. "I'm a girl who likes thrills and speed, and golf always seemed like a sport that . . . well . . . just didn't provide that stuff."

Looking at Jennifer in her leather jacket and fierce-looking motorcycle boots, I could see how golf might have been a hard sell, but when Greg defiantly bought her a set of clubs for her birthday, Jennifer found she couldn't resist the challenge of trying to beat Greg at his own game. Besides, Greg had also bought her four lessons and a roll of tokens for the ball machine. A few weeks later, much to Greg's astonishment, Jennifer announced that she felt ready to venture onto the course. "We had an awesome time," Jen confessed. "Greg was impressed with what I had learned and I was able to appreciate like never before how well he played, because I finally understood the game."

My take-away from this, which I shared with the couples at our next nine-and-dine: Guys, when all else fails give your gal a present. And gals, remember that men *just want you to say yes.* 🙂

A husband should never try to teach his wife to play golf or drive a car. A wife should never try to teach her husband to play bridge.

—Harvey Penick

CONSIDER CLUB MEMBERSHIP

To join or not to join . . . that is the question my husband and I keep turning over. Joining a country club would offer us, as golfers, access to a fantastic course and a unique social network. But it's expensive and somewhat limiting, too. How to decide? Here are the arguments for and against, as I see them:

Pros	Cons
beautiful, well-maintained course	you pay handsomely for it
tons of great tee times	. . . if you're a guy
never crowded	same people all the time
top instructors	uptight members
awesome pro shop	short on patterned skorts
spiffy carts	extra fees
decent caddies	tipping required
playing the same holes lowers your handicap	playing the same holes gets really boring
top-notch restaurant	spending minimums
no need to go anywhere else	can't afford to go anywhere else
competitive leagues	mean girls
great for professional networking	can't let your hair down

We do play a lot, and I can see playing even more if we were to join. Still those fees are steep. Next year, maybe. ☺

HOW TO NAVIGATE THE MEMBER-GUEST

The biggest social event of the year at any country club is the Member-Guest, where those who've "arrived" show off by inviting nonmember friends to their club for a weekend of lavish entertainment. A round or two of tournament golf anchors the event, but for non-golf-playing spouses there's plenty in the way of dining, dancing, and drinking. "Tee gifts," door prizes, and tournament awards can be worth thousands of dollars.

The costs of participating, however, are rather high. The golf alone can run hundreds of dollars, let alone the dinner and bar tab. Traditionally, whoever does the inviting bears the costs, the idea being, you as guest will likely reciprocate at your club when the opportunity presents itself. But if you don't belong to a club, you can offer to share in the expense. You might offer to pick up the entry fee, or cover any extraneous food and drink charges. Certainly you should cover any purchases you make in the pro shop.

If you feel uncomfortable with the expenses or the implied burden of returning the favor, it's probably best to decline the invitation. Otherwise, however, have a ball—because it just doesn't get better than this.

PLAY NINE, THEN DINE

Jumbo Lump Crab Cake
Shellfish Fettuccini alla Vodka
New York Sirloin
Caesar Salad
Steamed Shrimp Platter
Vegetable Stir Fry

nd that's just this week's nine-and-dine menu at Richter Park, our municipal course whose eighteenth hole features a lovely outdoor terrace restaurant.

Nine-and-dines are a growing phenomenon in both public and private golf venues. They combine a nine-hole round of golf with a relaxed evening of drinks and dinner, the idea being to induce golfers and their spouses to get to know other golf-inclined couples. It's a fabulous deal, certainly in terms of cost: greens fees, cart use, and dinner total at Richter about $35 per person (drinks are extra, natch). During the summer months, my husband and I have come to really enjoy the late-day ritual of teeing off around 4 p.m., playing until twilight, and then mingling on the terrace with the rest of our foursome and their mates.

What I really like is the noncompetitive aspect: Everyone, whether they play golf or not, is welcome to sign up. This allows spouses who are tentative participants to join in the fun, even if they just ride around in the cart with us before dinner. For some women, the nine-and-dine is the perfect entrée to taking up golf.

I'd have to point out, too, that the nine-and-dines have introduced us to people whose friendship we enjoy off the course as much as on it. One couple we met at Richter—she's celebrating her fortieth year as a flight attendant, and he's retired—are now fixtures in our lives, friends who join us at the theatre, at our home for dinner, at wine tastings, and perhaps on our next barge trip through France.

But if I'm to be totally honest, I must also admit I love the nine-and-dines for what they reveal about people I've known only as golfers. I was shocked to learn, for instance, that the most conservative, prim-faced lady in our league was married to the Lothario of our links, the one rumored to be intimate with some of the other wives. And the guy with the 4 handicap, who so impressed me during our round? He turned out to be a very bland and painfully shy accountant. It just goes to show, you can learn a lot about someone over nine holes, but you can learn even more over two glasses of chardonnay.

So keep an eye out for those sign-up sheets. Nine-and-dines are quite likely to offer you a social life that transcends the game. ☺

INDULGE YOUR FASHION FETISH

The crowd presses up against the runway, enthralled as lanky ladies sashay up and down in flirty little skirts and form-fitting capris. Photographers jostle for position and journalists scribble notes. Along comes a blonde in a body-hugging, racer-back minidress in hot pink. The throng erupts in applause.

Paris? New York? Try Orlando, Florida. This is the PGA Merchandise Show, a trade event held annually at the Fashion Gallery, and it is definitely not your mother's wardrobe on display. Golf wear and accessories occupy a full 6,300 square feet of floor space, which goes to show how big a player golf has become in fashion circles. Cutting-edge designers like Stella McCartney and Claudia Romana, Calvin Klein and Donna Karan ensure that golf styles for women keep women buying more golf apparel.

My own golf wardrobe occupies a walk-in closet. This is because about a year ago, my skorts and polos began to outnumber my skirts and blouses. And because I've never met a sparkly golf accessory I didn't love, and because I have a thing, definitely, for caps and bags, I needed shelves. *Lots* of them. (All I can say, to those who accuse me of going overboard with my golf purchases, is that my buying habits are keeping a universe of golf entrepreneurs in business.) A brief inventory:

Shoes: A multitiered rack currently holds eighteen pairs of size-seven soft-spike shoes, in as many different colors. The styles range from the classic black-and-white FootJoy saddle to the edgy Puma Golf Cat with its contrasting suede and leather and a removable kiltie. There's my prized pair of leopard-print Walter Genuins and T-strap Aerogreens in multihued woven leather. That's to name a few. Of course my husband calls me the Imelda Marcos of golf. And that doesn't bother me one bit.

Shirts: I'm definitely not draconian when it comes to dressing for golf but there's one country club rule I do agree with: the collared shirt. T-shirts are fine for the range, but I just like the finished look of a collar on the course. My polos—and I've got about thirty—are all fitted and mostly sleeveless. Several are halters or racer-backs. Lacoste is my favorite brand, partly because of the fit and the quality, but largely because I'm such a fan of the family who runs the company. Lacoste sponsors some of my favorite golfers, too: Cristie Kerr and Lorena Ochoa both wear the little green crocodile. On occasion I'll wear Ralph Lauren, not because I like the oversize pony logo but because nobody designs a better halter-top.

Skorts: Why wear a skirt or a pair of shorts when you can have the best of both? Skorts give you the coverage of shorts but the flirtatious look of a skirt. I have dozens in high-tech fabrics from Adidas and Nikes that I wear for casual rounds, and I have a sleek black Tommy Hilfiger that looks decidedly urban. But what I really love are my Lily Pulitzers. With their bright tropical colors and grosgrain ribbon trim, they're pure eye candy. A Lily skort always makes my round brighter.

Accessories: Where else but a golf course does a girl get to wear gloves? Gloves, like hats, complete an ensemble, and you can never have too many. I'm partial to pastels; I often coordinate my gloves with my hats, which range in style from caps to fedoras, Stetsons to bucket hats. I think a matching bag is a nice touch, so I've got several. As for jewelry, I never leave the house without a bejeweled ball marker. I've got a dozen or so in different shapes, each embellished with Swarovski crystal. Just holding one can make me happy, no matter how high my score is. I'm pretty sure, actually, that they bring me luck.

I could stage a runway show of my own, it's true. But as I see it, we owe it to ourselves, and all those men out there, to look better-than-par even when (*especially* when) our game isn't.☺

GOLF GUYS I ADMIRE:

Ian Poulter

I'm a huge Ian Poulter fan and have been since first noticing his lime-green retro look at the 2006 Masters. An awesome golfer by any standard (Seven wins on the European Tour and a second place showing at the 2009 Player's Championship), Poulter may be our generation's Lee Trevino or Chi Chi Rodriguez, giving the serious guys a run for their money on the tees and having great fun while he's at it.

He's on my list of favorites because he is an out-and-out style star. It's no surprise he's launched his own line of clothing, since the Englishman never misses an opportunity to make fashion statements on the course, famously dressing head-to-toe in pink for the U.S. Open and in patriotic Union Jack pants for the British Open. Poulter played the 2005 British Open wearing trousers emblazoned with the tournament's symbol, the claret jug, causing multiple-Open-champion Seve Ballesteros to quip to reporters, "That's the closest he'll ever get to it." (In fact, in 2008, Poulter came in second, trailing winner Padraig Harrington by four strokes.)

Plenty of fans have been annoyed or even offended by Poulter's wardrobe choices. But however you feel about his ensembles, you have to admit: They give us something to gab about each time Poulter plays.

For those of you golf girls who like your men in pink, I've got just the drink: the Pink Poulter. Conjured by my friend Gemma and inspired by Ian, it's the pause that refreshes when you're hot and bothered by someone whose sense of humor on the course has gone missing.

PINK POULTER

2 cl Citron vodka
2 cl cranberry juice
1 cl sugar syrup
Champagne

Mix vodka, cranberry juice, and sugar syrup, and pour into a champagne coupe or flute. Fill with champagne or a dry sparkling wine.

"I don't like the way most people dress on the golf course .... There are too many boring characters out there who don't have much spark apart from their golf game. My sporting heroes were the likes of Ronnie O'Sullivan, Muhammad Ali, Pelé, and of course the late Payne Stewart, all colourful characters."

—Ian Poulter

PREP FOR SUCCESS

Oh, *what* to wear? Dress codes in golf have eased to the point where . . . well, where I think we need to agree on some guidelines. But what those might be is a topic that stirs considerable controversy—particularly where female players, both pro and recreational, are concerned.

There are those, for instance, who feel it's time to distance golf from all that preppy design that has prevailed in the sport for *sooo* long. You know—the spouting-whale motifs and relentless pink-and-green color schemes. During the second round of the Fields Open, Michelle Wie took this to mean she could wear what looked like a Target tank top. Now I'm a huge Michelle Wie fan; I think she looks good in almost anything. But tank tops on golf courses? I don't approve. I'm fine with sleeveless polos; I'm fine with *backless* polos. Still, I think a collar should be mandatory. It has to do with looking pulled-together, not with how much skin is exposed.

I admit, I've come full circle on the appropriateness of the preppy look. Born and raised in Greenwich, Connecticut, fiefdom of preppiness, I can claim to know a thing or two about it. After countless summers spent sailing on Long Island Sound and vacationing on Nantucket, I developed, shortly after high school, a strong resistance to Kelly green and Lily Pulitzer pink. At the mere sight of madras and argyle, I'd break out in a rash. I expressed outright disdain for Lacoste alligators and prancing Polo ponies. And it went on like that for a while. I lived in Manhattan and Paris and, in preppy protest, wore nothing but black. It was my uniform, and I was proud of it.

But then, in Paris, I took up golf. And the whole whimsy of the sport, played out on Kelly green courses with Pulitzer-pink-clad clubs, clashed with my dull fashion palette. Those saturated hues and whimsical logos that identify all preppies, no matter where they live and work and play . . . are just so at home on the course. Those bright plaids and childish patterns—who can resist?

Turns out, not me. Preppy is back in a big way, both on and off the course. It's a little bit retro and a lot sexier. Now that even hip-hop stars espouse it, it's taken on a *gangsta* flair.

Preppy + Gangsta = Prepsta. That's the look. And— preppy that I am—I think it should be.

RECOVER FROM MORTAL EMBARRASSMENT

We were playing at Richter Park, our municipal course (and often cited as one of the top twenty-five public courses in the country), on a beautiful Friday evening in July, and we were the last foursome, finishing up our round as twilight turned to dusk. As we approached the eighteenth hole, shouting and laughter spilled from the terraced café that overlooks the last green. It was a bachelor party, and the guests, well on their way to total inebriation, had taken up viewing positions on the balcony. Since the "official entertainment" hadn't yet arrived, they were amusing themselves by commenting on the players as they came in.

One could sense from way down the fairway that the comments were not flattering. I managed a decent drive, just short of the green. Feeling the collective gaze from the balcony, I pulled out my sand wedge and sized up my last approach shot. Something would go terribly wrong, I just knew. Amazingly, though, I hit a chip shot right onto the green about four feet from the hole. My captive audience roared with admiration.

I felt more than relieved; I felt great. And as I tend to do when I'm feeling at the top of my game, I walked onto the green swishing my putter jauntily back and forth, confident I was one stroke from finishing.

Somehow, though, on the way to that last stroke, my swishing putter swished in slightly the wrong direction and wound up between my ankles, just as I took a step. I stumbled forward, practically knocking the flag out on my way down, and landed sprawled on my hands and knees.

You can well imagine how my audience at the café reacted.

I got up, smoothed my skirt down, and attempted to get a grip on both my club and my dignity. The crowd hushed. I tapped the ball in the direction of the cup. It rolled past. The boys on the balcony hooted. I tapped it again—and it stopped at the lip. To my eternal embarrassment, I actually three-putted that last hole.

Just recalling this makes my face heat up in humiliation. But I thought it worth sharing for two reasons: (1) you should really be careful with your putter, and (2) everybody, and I mean everybody, has had one of these moments or worse out on the course. Should it happen to you—*when* it happens to you—just remember that you're in excellent company. ☺

Epilogue

HOW I SHAVED FIVE STROKES OFF MY GAME

hree years playing at this sport has confirmed for me something few women realize: We have the right stuff. The very characteristics men criticize in us—our methodical approach, our sense of caution, our precision and finesse—groom us to be excellent golfers. Much is made (by men) of our inferior driving ability, but anyone who's spent serious time on her game recognizes that being able to read a course and play strategically will consistently result in fewer strokes than being able to pull off a 300-yard bomber. We girls know when to hold back; if we tend not to "go for it," it's because we won't let ourselves get in that sort of desperate position in the first place. Look at Lorena Ochoa: She can drive like a man, but wins because she plays like a woman, setting up her shots methodically so she avoids having to take crazy risks. To be sure, our victories are less stunning—no Tiger-like pyrotechnics, no Mickelson miracles, no Daly-esque dramas—but we get the job done. And well.

This may explain why women's golf initially had trouble finding an audience. Viewers love, after all, golfers who risk it all to dig themselves out of desperate situations. But we girls offer something else that viewers, both men and women, can appreciate: Let's just call it eye candy. Professional women golfers like Natalie Gulbis understand that it's their feminine physicality as much as their athleticism that attracts attention. And what's wrong with that? There's no such thing as bad attention if you're a woman on the pro circuit: The more viewers who tune in (for whatever reason), the more sponsors take notice;

the more visible women golfers become, the more women join the sport. Growing the sport, however it's accomplished, is a win-win for both sexes.

Beyond native ability and intrinsic beauty, however, the most important thing we bring to the game is our attitude. When Michelle Wie got a lot of air time for playing with the PGA qualifiers, a number of (male) sports writers claimed veteran LPGA players were "miffed" at being eclipsed by someone who'd never even played in their tournaments. This was pure invention, the sort of thing guys would think, obsessed with winning and losing as they are. And it blinded them to what was *really* noteworthy about this young woman: Despite having little chance of making the cut, let alone winning, she chose to compete with the sport's top players *because it was fun*! She wasn't in it to win, but to learn. Like most women, Michelle Wie finds playing golf highly enjoyable whether she's "good enough" or not. Whereas men will give up golf because they're not winning, women will take it up, and keep playing, because they feel they have nothing to lose. And merely by playing more often, with more joy, they get better. Men, poor things, just can't seem to adopt that mindset.

I enjoy playing whether my handicap is 34 or 20 or 12 or 0. I suffer my share of bad shots, but I never focus on them. I'm taking great pleasure in my swing these days, because I know it's going to be solid, effective, and consistent. Mastering the swing has been really satisfying. It makes me feel as if I'm ready to take on the more competitive leagues, and play the more challenging courses—perhaps the Winged Foot courses in Mamaroneck, New York, or the Pete and Alice Dye course in Pound Ridge, or even the desert courses of Phoenix, Arizona. I flirt with the notion of playing Ballybunion in County Kerry, Ireland, and of course, Carnoustie and St. Andrews in Scotland. The nice thing is, I don't have to be in any desperate hurry to play there, because in golf as in no other sport, getting older isn't an issue. With every year I play, I get better—without having to worry I'm going to hurt myself trying. I've just got to work on my sand escapes.

My enjoyment goes beyond the physical, too. Lately I've come to see that golf represents a key networking opportunity for me, one that men have always exploited but from which women have been excluded. I joined Women on Course, an online golf club for gals that organizes networking events both on and off the course. Donna Hoffman, the television producer who started the club, brings golfers together through contests, food-and-wine events, club fittings, and golf clinics. "Rather than focus on the time and commitment it takes to achieve a low handicap," she observes, "we highlight the business and social benefits of the game." My priorities exactly!

Most surprisingly, however, I've come to perceive that my enjoyment of golf has changed my overall outlook. This is no small thing for me. I've always seen myself as a realist, something of a cynic, even; only on the golf course did I get to feel lighthearted and optimistic. Yet by teaching me to value a swing that feels pure and clean, a drive that lofts high and true, a putt that sinks as though pulled gravitationally to the hole, golf has taught me a sense of wonderment, one that accompanies me off the course in everything I do. I tend to see the glass half full now, rather than half empty. I focus on the moments of grace, when things go unexpectedly, magically right. I believe that, so long as I enjoy what I do, I will grow and improve at it—an inspiring belief if ever there was one. This I owe to golf.

So if I've become a golf evangelist, you can understand why. Yes, it's a great outing with friends, a beautiful way to spend an afternoon. I love the socializing; I love the shopping. But when I meet someone who mentions those glorious moments, of seeing the ball fly on a perfect trajectory toward the dazzling green around the pin, I tap into the joy, and wish only that I had taken up golf sooner, that it might have opened my eyes earlier. At the very least, I figure, I can evangelize. The world would be a better place if more of us saw it with the wonderment it warrants. ☺

OFF-THE-COURSE CONNECTIONS

Have a question about the rules? Eager to connect with other women golfers? Looking for a crystal-studded ball marker? All your answers are online: Just Google "women's golf" or "ladies' golf" and you'll see what I mean. Below are some of my regular haunts, but with new sites and blogs coming online every day, I'm still discovering favorites. You can always find an up-to-date list of the best on the Web at www.golfgirlmedia/links.

Sites and Organizations

LPGA: www.lpga.com

Ladies Links fore Golf: www.LL4G.com

Golf Digest Women: www.golfdigestwomen.com

Executive Women's Golf Association: www.ewga.com

Cybergolf Women: www.cybergolf.com/womensgolf

Women on Course: www.womenoncourse.com/

Ladies Golf Journey: www.womenoncourse.com/

Blogs

Golf Girl's Diary: www.thegolfgirl.blogspot.com

Golf Babes: www.golf-babes.com

Mostly Harmless: mlyhlss.blogspot.com/

Hound Dog: www.hounddoglpga.com

Real Women Golf: realwomengolf.blogspot.com/

Pink Diva Golf: pinkdivagolf.blogspot.com/

GolfGal: www.golfgal-blog.com/

Golf Equipment and Apparel

Lacoste: www.lacoste.com

Lady Golf: www.ladygolf.com

Golf Sophisticate: www.golfsophisticate.com

Sweet Lies: www.sweetliesgolf.com

Tail: www.tailinc.com

Golf 'n Gals: www.golfngals.com

Trigelle: www.trigelle.com

Lija: www.lijastyle.com

Puma: http://golf.puma.com/us/en/

Acknowledgments

This book was born of my passion for golf, so I'd first like to thank those who ignited that passion: the friends who patiently played with me when I was an arch beginner, and encouraged me not to give up; the instructor who always found creative ways to help me improve, but never allowed me to lose sight of the fun; and the professional golfers who inspired me from the fairways and greens, in person and on the small screen. To these women (and men), I offer the most heartfelt thanks.

I would especially like to thank my golf girl sisters, June Moris and Colleen Hannigan, and my indentical twin, Cathleen Farr, who discovered this game with me and will always be my fave foursome. Thanks to Ed McCallen, an instructor whose patience is exemplary and whose humor made every lesson delightful. Special thanks are also in order for the women of the LPGA, LET, and Futures Tours whose dedication to playing golf at the highest level is a huge part of why we recreational golfers are driven to play better. Watching these ladies week after week is endlessly entertaining, extremely inspiring, and often enlightening.

Putting this book together was a collaborative effort and involved many different skill sets. I'd like to thank my stellar team at Lark Productions, agent Lisa DiMona and editor Melinda Marshall, for their insight, input, and support. At Stewart, Tabori & Chang, my thanks go to my editor Jennifer Levesque, designer Pamela Geismar, marketing aces Kerry Liebling and Julia Coblentz, and publicist Claire Bamundo for their fine, creative work

Finally, I'd like to thank the readers of my blog, Golf Girl's Diary. Your daily comments and emails are what keep me writing, and ultimately turned my golf blogging adventure into this book.